The Ramesseum

Wilhelm Spiegelberg, James Edward Quibell, R F. E. Paget

SAQQARA. PTAH-HOTEP'S SON.

EGYPTIAN RESEARCH ACCOUNT,

1896.

THE RAMESSEUM.

BY

J. E. QUIBELL.

WITH TRANSLATIONS AND COMMENTS BY

W. SPIEGELBERG.

AND

THE TOMB OF PTAH-HETEP.

COPIED BY

R. F. E. PAGET AND A. A. PIRIE.

WITH COMMENTS BY

F. LL. GRIFFITH.

LONDON:

BERNARD QUARITCH, 15, PICCADILLY, W.

1898.

LONDON:
PRINTED BY WILLIAM CLOWES AND SONS, Limited,
STAMFORD STREET AND CHARING CROSS.

CONTENTS.

CHAPTER I.

SECT. PAGE

1. Introduction 1
2. General character of the work 2

CHAPTER II.

XIITH DYNASTY.

3. Tomb of ivory boy 3
4. Tomb of Se-hetep-ab-ra 4
5. Lesser tombs 4

XVIIITH DYNASTY.

6. Bricks, and earlier temples 5
7. Sculptures of Deir el Bahri, &c. . . . 5

CHAPTER III.

XIXTH DYNASTY.

8. Stone temple of Ramesseum 5
9. Foundation deposits 6
10. Brick galleries 6
11. The plan 7
12. Oil and wine jars 8
13. Scene of the tree-goddess 8
14. Trial pieces of sculptors 9
15. Lintel of Ramessu III 9

CHAPTER IV.

XXIIND DYNASTY.

16. Buildings re-used for burials 9
17. Tomb of Iuf-en-Amen 9
18. Tomb of Hes-bast 10
19. Tomb of Nekht-ef-Mut 10
20. Scattered objects, XXIInd dynasty . . . 11
21. Funerary chapels 11
22. Heart scarabs, beads, &c. 12
23. Ushabtiu 12
24. Use of iron 13
25. Pottery 13
26. Hoard of coins 13

CHAPTER V.

THE INSCRIPTIONS BY DR. W. SPIEGELBERG.

SECT. PAGE

27. Pl. IV. Ramesseum fragments 14
28. Pls. VI–IX. Tomb of Se-hetep-ab-ra . . 14
29. Pl. X. Steles 15
30. „ XI. Brick stamps 15
31. „ XII. Jar sealings 15
32. „ XIII. Sculptures, various . . . 16
33. „ XIV. Lintel of Ramessu III . . . 16
34. „ XVI. Coffin of Nekht-ef-Mut . . . 16
35. Pls. XVII–XIX. Short Inscriptions . . 16
36. „ XX–XXI. Wooden steles . . . 17
37. Pl. XXII. Tomb sculptures 18
38. Pls. XXIII–XXIV. Sculptures of Nekht-ef-Mut 18
39. „ XXV–XXVI. Cartonnage . . . 18
40. Pl. XXVII. Steles of XVIII–XXII dyn. . 19
41. „ XXVIII. Cartonnage of Hor . . 20
42. „ XXIX. Tuy and Zed-thuti-auf-ankh . 20
43. „ XXX. Scarabs 20
44. „ XXXA. Chapter 125, &c. 20

THE TOMB OF PTAH-HETEP.

BY F. LL. GRIFFITH, M.A., F.S.A.

45. Character and position 25
46. Previous publications 25
47. Subjects of walls 26
48. Pl. XXXVII. Sides of doorway. . . . 26
49. „ XXXV. Ptah-hetep with servants . . 27
50. Pls. XXXII–XXXIII. Games, vineyard, hunting, and river scenes 27
51. Pls. XXXI–XXXIII. Ptah-hetep receiving produce 29
52. Pls. XXXIV–XXXV. Offerings from estates, &c. 30
53. Pl. XXXVI. Preparing and bringing offerings 31
54. Pls. XXXVIII–XLI. Left-hand door. . 31
55. Outer doorway 32
56. Second false door 33
57. Date and offices of Ptah-hetep . . . 33

INDEX 35

LIST OF PLATES.

THE RAMESSEUM.

BY J. E. QUIBELL.

I. Plan of the Ramesseum.
II. Photographs.
III. XIIth dynasty tomb.
IV. List of proper names, XXIInd dynasty.
V. Fragments of Cheta battle-scene.
VI–IX. Tomb of Se-hotep-ab-ra, XIIth dynasty.
X. Stelae.
XI. Brick stamps.
XII. Pottery.
XIII. Blocks of Thothmes III.
XIV. Lintel of Rameses III.
XV. Foundation deposits, Rameses II.
XVI. Cartonnage of Nekht-ef-mut.
XVII. Small objects of Nekht-ef-mut.
XVIII. Leather braces, XXIInd dynasty.
XIX. Canopic jars.
XX. Scene of tree-goddess, etc.
XXI. Wooden stelae, XXIInd dynasty.
XXII. Sandstone slabs, XXIInd dynasty.
XXIII. Inscriptions on sandstone.
XXIV, XXV. Cartonnage, XXIInd dynasty.
XXVI. Inscriptions on wooden coffins.
XXVII. Sandstone stelae.
XXVIII. Cartonnage of Hor.
XXIX. Inscription of Tuy, etc.
XXX. Scarabs.
XXX A. Cartonnage of Hor, etc.

TOMB OF PTAH-HETEP.

BY MISS PIRIE AND MISS PAGET.

XXXI. East wall, south end.
XXXII. East wall, north end.
XXXIII. East wall.
XXXIV. South wall.
XXXV. South and north walls.
XXXVI. North wall.
XXXVII. Doorway.
XXXVIII. West wall, middle.
XXXIX. West wall, south end.
XL. West wall, north end.
XLI. West wall, middle.

CHAPTER I.

1. The Ramesseum—the great temple built by Rameses II, where future ages should worship him—is one of the most impressive ruins of Thebes. Though not so perfect as the temple of Rameses III at Medinet Habu, yet, through its granite colossus lying dethroned at the entrance, its stately colonnade, the great battle-scenes sculptured on its walls, and the unusual view of a temple deprived of its surrounding shell, this half-destroyed pile possesses a singular interest. Even of those tourists who have been led to the top, and who, walking over the vast roofing beams, have peered down into the avenues of columns, few realise how large a space was originally covered by the establishment of Rameses the Great. Beyond the remaining hall of columns, now without any side walls, lie the foundations of the lesser chambers which enclosed the halls on each side and at the back, and, stretching far beyond these, are the great brick arches or tunnels which formed the store-houses of a complex religious establishment which drew its revenues from distant estates, and maintained an army of ministrants.

No regular digging had, till we arrived, been undertaken here, and the chance of finding some library of the priests made the site attractive. On the northern side some chambers still retained their vaulted roofs. These, when cleared out and divided by rough cross-walls into separate compartments, made a possible dwelling-place; here we lived during the winter. Two of the long chambers or tunnels served for our party; a third was devoted to the workmen, and in the fourth lived the families of two of the men, who had been allowed to bring their wives. Great difficulty had been foreseen in dealing with the people of the neighbouring village of Qurneh, who have throughout this century lived chiefly by illicit dealing in antiquities. The wages of honest labour have remained at 2 P.T. (5*d.*) a day, but an ever-increasing number of the people have made vastly greater profits by labour more or less connected with tomb-robbing.

We accordingly brought up from Quft and Ballas about forty of our old workmen to be used as a guard and for the more important work, and these more trusty workmen Dr. Petrie kindly left to me at first, taking on his own work the local men. These proved to be even worse than we had expected; the habit of thieving was so engrained in them, and they were so held in the toils of the dealers, that not even the heavy backsheesh, given on their finds, could tempt them to be honest, even to their own profit. A certain number of objects were stolen and taken over to the dealers at Luxor, and from them soon passed into the hands of tourists. It was found necessary to discharge almost all the Qurneh men, and to rely entirely upon our old workmen from Quft; besides these, I enlisted a group of men from a village about two hours south. After the dismissal of the local men we had no further losses. Smaller dealers, it is true, sat every day by the wells at which our men drew water, and offered them large prices for anything they would sell, and every market day was a danger; but hardly any attempts were made to molest the faithful men, and at the end of the season, by taking care to travel in large groups, they all got home in safety. Still, a large part of the winter's energies was spent in the continual struggle with the dealers; their success would have meant the destruction of the scientific value of all our work. It is a pleasure, therefore, to recognise the good feeling of one dealer, Mohammed Mohassib of Luxor, who refused to buy anything stolen from us on the ground that he would not make a profit from the robbery of his friends. And, whenever our other dealer friend, Girgis, came from Qeneh, his actions were above suspicion, as we have always found them.

I have to gratefully acknowledge the assistance of

several people. In Egypt, Miss Pirie and my sister gave invaluable aid in many ways; and, during the short time he was with us, Mr. J. G. Milne was exceedingly helpful to me. Our friend, Mr. P. E. Newberry, who was a resident at Luxor during our stay at Thebes, spared neither time nor trouble in his efforts to increase our comfort and assist our work. I should find it difficult to express adequately my sense of his unwearied and thoughtful kindness; the value of his help, as much in our work as in personal matters, cannot be over-estimated. In England, Miss Griffith, Miss Murray, Miss Whidborne, Dr. Walker, and Mr. Herbert Thompson, have shared in much of the labour of arrangement for exhibition, and in the dispersal of the different objects to museums. Mr. Christie has done many of the drawings. Special thanks are due to Dr. Spiegelberg, who gave us much help both in Egypt and in England. At Thebes he often came to us in the evening, after his own work of searching for graffiti, and gave us rapid translations of such inscriptions as we had found. In the following summer he came to London and worked over the material at University College. He has aided me in the writing of this account, and all translations of inscriptions and comments on them are due to him. For plans, descriptions of finds, etc., and the work of excavation, I am alone responsible. It should be stated that, while using the English method of transcription for English readers, Dr. Spiegelberg retains his preference for the more rigorous German methods. Nor must I forget to mention the extreme rapidity with which he has written his description of the plates. The arrears of work from the very heavy Naqada year intruded upon the time which should have been given by me to the Ramesseum, so that when the plates reached Dr. Spiegelberg very few weeks could be allowed him if the book were to be published without further delay.

Not all the material found is published in this volume. One large section, the Ostraca, is being edited by Dr. Spiegelberg in a separate publication, and the fragments of papyri, the tiny remnants of the Ramesseum library, are being worked over by the same hand. It should also be mentioned that a considerable part of the Ramesseum was excavated by Dr. Petrie, using funds provided by Mr. Jesse Haworth and Mr. Martyn Kennard; the material so found is published here, while such parts of the temples of Siptah etc. as I worked are taken over by Dr. Petrie into his "Six Temples."

2. The brick buildings consist of long chambers about 12 feet wide. Although the roofs remain in only a few places, the side walls, 4½ feet thick, were generally in good condition; it was therefore easy to get the work done by measure instead of by time. Two or four men were generally put to work together; they cleared out a section of a chamber about 12 feet long, throwing all the earth behind them; when one section had been cleared and examined they passed on to another, and threw the soil from this into the space left by their first task. The whole of the ground was thus turned over; all the tomb shafts found were also dug out. This kind of work was more expensive than digging a cemetery like that of Naqada, because of the depth of brick-rubbish that had to be cleared away before the layer could be reached in which remains of interest occurred (*v.* PL. II, 3). The layer of debris of roof and walls was often 8 feet thick, and never contained anything of importance. It was some compensation that in these open chambers and shallow wells there was no risk of burying men alive, as there often is in deep well work. The character of the finds was very uniform; each chamber much like the next. In the upper layer were ushabtis and fragments of cartonnage and wooden coffins, all thrown up by plunderers from the tomb-wells. Near the floor of the chambers were fragments of wine- and oil-jars, etc., some of them inscribed. Under the floor were two classes of tomb-wells. The rarer class were large oblong shafts 12 × 3 feet at the top, skew to the line of the building, and sometimes running under the walls; evidently therefore of earlier date than the temple. The wells of the more numerous class were much smaller, about 4 feet square, dug through the floor of the chambers, and most frequently close to one wall. They never ran under the walls, were not more than 8 feet deep, and often had a wall about 3 feet high, and half a brick thick, surrounding their mouths. These little walls must have been built to keep the brick debris from falling down the well, which shows that these graves were made after the roofs had fallen in, and when the chambers were already full of rubbish. These, as well as the graves of the earlier period, were almost always robbed. In one group of chambers they had been robbed very thoroughly; hardly any ushabtis, beads, or pieces of cartonnage remained; these had probably been cleared out within this century, and by dealers. But in the shafts of most of these graves ushabtis were scattered, while only small parts of the wooden coffins remained. For ushabtis there has always been a market for the last eighty years, and dealers would

hardly leave them behind, so it may be that these tombs were cleared out in the last century, when, as Dr. Waldemar Schmidt suggested to me, graves would be opened to get timber. All these small graves seem to belong to a brief period, about the XXIInd dynasty. The names Sheshanq, Osorkon, Takeloth, were repeatedly found, but no names of earlier or later kings.

CHAPTER II.

3. The most important tomb of the XIIth dynasty period consisted of a long, oblong shaft, skew to the wall of one of the chambers (No. 5, Pl. I) and running under it. In the shaft were scattered two types of ushabtis, one of green glaze, another of clay painted yellow but not baked. These were of XXIInd dynasty style, as were also a wooden head from a coffin lid, some small wax figures of the four genii, and fragments of red leather braces.

At the bottom of the shaft, 13 feet down, two small chambers opened. These were cleared out and found to be empty. Lastly, the heap left in the middle of the shaft was removed, and in it, in a space about 2 feet square, was found a group of objects, some of which are shown in Pl. III.

First was a wooden box about 18 × 12 × 12 inches. It was covered with white plaster, and on the lid was roughly drawn in black ink the figure of a jackal. The box was about one third full of papyri which were in extremely bad condition, three quarters of their substance having decayed away; if a fragment of the material were pressed slightly between the finger and thumb it disappeared in a mere dust. But the papyrus was inscribed; characters apparently of the XIIth dynasty hieratic could be distinguished. The papyrus was packed with care and has been brought to England. It is too delicate even to be unfolded, but it is to be hoped that Mr. Griffith may, by copying what can be seen on one fold and then brushing or scraping this away, get access to the next and so make out much of the text.

In the box was also a bundle of reed pens, 16 inches long and a tenth of an inch in diameter, and scattered round it were a lot of small objects; parts of four ivory castanets (iii, 1, 2, 3) incised with the usual series of mythical creatures, a bronze uraeus entangled in a mass of hair, a cat and an ape in green glaze (5, 6), and a handful of beads. These comprised spherical beads in amethyst and agate, barrel-shaped in haematite and carnelian, glaze and carnelian beads of the shape of an almond, and one covered with minute crumbs of glaze. The green glaze object (7) like a cucumber in shape is not understood. There is one at Gizeh and another has lately been found in a XIIth dynasty grave at El Kab. (*Cf.* also Mission du Caire, Planche XXII.) The ivory piece (8) is pierced at the round end for the insertion of a handle; similar objects were found at Kahun (Kahun, VIII, 18), but their use is not known. The rude doll (9), without arms or legs, is made of a flat slip of wood ¼ inch thick, the painted cross-lines on the body seem to represent some plaid material. The next two dolls, with arms but cut off at the knees, are of limestone and glaze respectively (10, 11). A patch on the latter is covered, not with smooth glaze like the rest of the figure, but with minute grains of blue frit; this must be due to imperfect firing, and shows that the glaze was applied as a wash of ground frit. The same method is seen in the ushabtis of a far later period.

The figure of a dancer (12) is in wood; the girl wears a mask and holds a bronze serpent in each hand (*cf.* the canvas mask found at Kahun, Pl. VIII, 14). The doll (13) is in limestone, the ape (14) in blue glaze, the *dad* in ivory, and the coarse cup (16) in blue glaze, while the plain castanet (17), and the handle (?) with two lions engraved on it, are of ivory. Seeds of the dom palm and of balanites were also found here. A very curious fragment is the ivory boy with a calf upon his back (length 2 inches). Found alone this might have passed for Roman work, but the position can leave no doubt that all these objects are from one interment and of one date.

The history of the tomb would appear to be as follows. The XIIth dynasty interment was discovered and robbed long ago, perhaps by the workmen of Rameses II, the valuables being taken away and the other objects thrown out into the shaft and left. When the Ramesseum was ruined and had been given over to some families of the XXIInd dynasty as a cemetery, the ready-made shaft was again utilised; it was cleared out until the mouths of the chamber were reached, and in them the second burials were placed. At some later period these too were disturbed, but in neither of the two last instances was the bottom of the shaft reached: so that when we, after finding the chambers empty, cleared completely the ground between them, we found this patch covered with the remains of the first interment. There [illegible] angles to the colonnade. This passage had been covered by an arch, the spring of which could still be seen; it continued under the E. wall of the colonnade and was obviously much the older work. The passage [illegible] a facade of rock in which opened a tunnel 30 feet long. The brick walls of the passage had been plastered, whitewashed, and painted with a series of scenes executed in a rough and bold style (Pl. VI, VII, VIII, IX). These were copied for us by Miss Pirie under conditions requiring considerable nerve, for the walls of brick rubbish stood with almost vertical faces on two sides, and one of the pillars and another large block were poised on a mass of loose brick rubbish, inconveniently near. From Miss Pirie's careful coloured copies, now kept at University College, the outlines in the plates were transferred. The passage between the decorated walls contained a group of XIXth dynasty pots (XII, 7); (some of them filled with cloth and the so-called nitre) embedded in the debris, which had no doubt been put there when the site was levelled for building. But the tunnel in the rock was almost clear; a small Arab bowl and a little pottery lamp showed that the last visitors had been Arabs. Pieces of bone, broken pottery, and fragments of painted wooden coffins, lay upon the floor; mingled with them were about 400 ushabtis with the names Ankh . ef and Pa . du . amen. In the centre lay a large pot (XII, 5), which the robbers had filled with ushabtis of plain green glaze as if to take them away. Twenty feet further on was a small niche 3 feet above the ground; it was empty.

[illegible] VIII and IX are the south side, the seated figure of the deceased in VIII being nearest the tomb. The colours are put on boldly, the figures of [illegible] being not even surrounded by the usual black outline; the women are yellow, the men, animals, and the broad line at the base below the water line, red. The shield ornaments of the cabin on the boat in Pl. VII are alternately black and red with white wavy lines. The boats are red, except the last, in which Se-hotep-ab-ra is carried; this is black. The [illegible] under which the owner is seated is in black and yellow. It is curious that the sailors in the next boat face the bows, they have stopped paddling, and the sail is being set.

5. Another tomb of the XIIth dynasty—a shaft with two chambers—was found in chamber 32. The period was shown by spherical blue glaze beads, barrel-shaped blue glaze, barrel amethysts, discs of ostrich egg-shell, and one of the typical earthenware tables of offerings. Minute gold and silver beads showed that the interment had been a rich one. A glazed plaque of Thothmes III may have belonged to one of the robbers. There was no other sign of re-use.

Just below the great wall to the north was the facade of another tomb, the tunnel of which runs under the wall. There remained enough pottery to make the period certain. An eye in iron from the inlay of a coffin, proved that the tomb had been re-used and robbed again.

Another of these tombs with long subterranean passages leading to a chamber, ran under two of the Ramesseum store-houses (36 and 37). It was entered both from the facade end, and from a small well in the side of the next chamber, by which the later people had accidentally gained access. Two pots of the typical XXIInd dynasty shape (XII, 11) belonged to the later use. A small limestone table of offerings, and two pots of the "salad-mixer" shape, with some stands for pottery, and a large water-jar, were of Middle Empire types. There was also a fragment of a limestone stela, in very bad condition, on which could be traced part of the figure of a standing man wearing a leopard-skin over his shoulders, and leaning upon a staff; a dog's head appears below him.

Of the XIIIth dynasty is an alabaster lid of a kohl-vase (PL. XVIII), with the name *uas-taui*, perhaps *Ra. sekhem. uas. taui*, Sebekhotep II.

6. Bricks were often found in the Ramesseum walls stamped with the names of earlier kings—Amenhotep II, Hatshepsut, Thothmes III, Thothmes IV, and Akhenaten. A block, with the two cartouches of Thothmes IV, lay in colonnade 14. It had probably covered the small pit containing the foundation deposits. Even one of the great sandstone jackals of Amenhotep III had been re-used here, and the two temples of Amenhotep II and Thothmes IV, lying close by, doubtless served as quarries for Rameses. In the first court, west of the pylon, there were found, 12 feet from the gateway, and at a depth of 10 feet, two drums of pillars. They were below the level of the pylon, and, therefore, too far down to belong to the Ramesseum; they probably came from some earlier temple.

To this earlier temple may also belong a great well, 10 feet in diameter (I, 60), in which we reached water, but did not find the bottom. It was probably a well for water.

At two points foundation deposits were discovered, not under any walls of the building, but in the middle of chambers, and at a low level. The pottery (XII, 2) might well be of the XVIIIth dynasty, for it was closely similar to that of Amenhotep II. A bed of fine gravel had been laid down, and the pots arranged in it in a circular group, the thirty-seven little bowls (in one case) nested in one another, and vases of other shapes grouped round them. These are most probably the remains of an earlier building, to which the buried pillars mentioned above may also belong.

7. The most curious traces of the XVIIIth dynasty were, however, the limestone blocks from Deir-el-Bahri, re-used by Rameses II. These occurred both under the colonnade at the west of the building, where they were placed below the columns, and also in the stone walls to the south, where they were generally turned with the inscribed face inside. Most of the pieces were of uraeus border, as in the shrine of Anubis, but three were of scenes of offerings. The best were taken back to Hatshepsut's temple, after three thousand years' absence, to be worked into M. Naville's restoration.

The lintel with inscription of Thothmes III (XIII, 1) was found opposite a gateway (I, 30), where it had doubtless been re-used.

The stela of Beba (X, 1) is, by the style and names, probably of the early XVIIIth dynasty. It is of limestone, and was found in the south-east corner of the building on a thin limestone pavement a foot above the untouched desert. This was here the level of the Ramesseum floor. The four upper figures of Beba, his wife, and the deities, are in relief, and have been much damaged; the rest of the inscription is incised.

The fragment from the tomb of An-na (XXIII, 6), the stela of Sipa-iri (XXVII, 5), fragments of glaze of Amenhotep II and of Thothmes IV, and an alabaster kohl-vase of Thothmes II (PL. XVIII), complete the list of XVIIIth dynasty objects.

CHAPTER III.

XIXTH DYNASTY.

8. We devoted ourselves almost entirely to the brick chambers, to the exclusion of the stone temple, but some fallen blocks of the scene on the north side of the second pylon, omitted in Lepsius, were copied (PL. V), and the eastern end, where all the walls have been removed, was turned over. Here, fragments of red pottery statues were found similar to those from the lowest levels of Koptos, and to others found by M. Daressy at Medinet-Habu. There was no means of knowing whether these had belonged to the XIXth dynasty, or to a later time; there is a strong presumption that they are not earlier than the Ramesseum, as they were found only in the stone building, and not near to any early tombs.

Many fragments of Coptic pottery lay inside the area of the stone building; none at all outside the line of the sandstone walls, showing that the outer walls were probably still standing in Christian times. A small clearance was also made in the forecourt, which showed that there was once a row of pillars on the west side corresponding to the two on the east. The bases of these pillars might, as Mr. Petrie has pointed out, be now used to carry a buttress, which is much needed for preserving the wall that bears the inscription of the battle of Kadesh. This well-known scene is now in a very perilous state; the wall, like all the others in the building, was built in two faces, with no bonding between them. One face has now fallen, and the other is only held by the heavy roofing

[illegible]

9. Foundation deposits were found at three points (A, B, C, Map 2) in the western part of the building where the walls have been cleared away in past days, and only the trenches in which they stood remain; along these, we could work without risk of doing any damage. At several other points where the cross-walls meet the long walls the deposits no doubt remain and, I hope, always will remain, undisturbed. The first trace of a deposit was found at the N.W. corner. Here lay a great sandstone block; underneath it, and with its edge just visible, was a small pit which we cleared out. It was about 5 feet deep, and of the same diameter, and had been entirely robbed. On getting into this pit, and looking up, one saw that the great block was inscribed on its under-side with the two cartouches of Rameses II incised, and painted yellow. A tile of green glaze was found a few feet away, doubtless dropped when the rest of the deposit was taken.

In the opposite corner, the S.W., we had better fortune. Again appeared the large block, nearly covering the little well, but the well was this time filled with clean sand instead of brick debris. Near the surface lay a block of sandstone, painted white and quite clean; on it were the names of Rameses incised, and painted yellow (XV, 13 and photographed II, 10); round it were a score of pots (14, 19, 22, 21, 18) and at the south edge the wooden brick mould (17). Half way down the hole was a floor of eight large mud bricks, neatly chipped to fit the space; upon this lay two blue glaze tiles (XV, 5) with gold-leaf cartouches upon a backing of plaster. The bulk of the deposit was, however, below the brick floor. Here, scattered through the sand were a wooden hoe (20), two wooden bowls (11) painted blue and with traces of cartouches, one plain blue [illegible], and knife, with the gilt foil, and sixteen small [illegible] of pottery (22). Besides these there were many small pieces of glaze, models of hands, calves' heads, [illegible] with [illegible] legs tied together (XV, 9), legs of [illegible] (10), seeds (7), and cartouches (3). A few of [illegible] models were in silver and gold foil. The glaze was in four colours, red, violet, blue, and white. There was no apparent reason in the number of objects of each colour, as will be seen from this table,

—	Red.	Violet.	Blue.	White.	Silver.	Gold.	Total.
Hand	[illegible]	[illegible]	[illegible]	[illegible]	[illegible]	[illegible]	[illegible]
Calf-head	[illegible]	[illegible]	[illegible]	[illegible]	[illegible]	[illegible]	[illegible]
Seed	[illegible]	[illegible]	[illegible]	[illegible]	[illegible]	..	[illegible]
Ox-leg	[illegible]	[illegible]	[illegible]	[illegible]	[illegible]	..	[illegible]
Ox	[illegible]	[illegible]	[illegible]	[illegible]	..	..	[illegible]
(Ra-user-maat)	[illegible]	[illegible]	[illegible]	..	..	..	[illegible]
(Ra-messu)	[illegible]	[illegible]	[illegible]	..	..	..	[illegible]

but the numbers of each class are about equal, except the two cartouches, which together equal the number of each other class.

In the third corner that we examined (I, c), the arrangement was much the same. The painted block with cartouches in yellow, with the larger vases, a granite corn-rubber, and four model bronze tools (8, 12), were above the brick floor; below it were small bowls, some broken pottery, three granite corn-rubbers, a bone from a calf's foot, a fragment of malachite, a semicircular plaque of alabaster with the two cartouches in black ink, four bronze knives, and two of the blue glaze tiles. The pieces of glaze were less numerous.

—	Red.	Violet.	Blue.	White.	Total.
Hand	6	..	3	4	13
Calf-head	2	2	6	2	12
Seed	8	2	7	3	20
Ox-leg	2	..	8	3	13
Ox	1	2	1	4	8
(Ra-user-maat)	..	3	3	..	6
(Ra-messu)	1	3	1	..	5
					77

The glazes in both deposits were of good quality and very distinctive colour.

10. But the chief monuments of this period, after the stone work, are the brick buildings themselves. The walls are very thick, generally 46 inches, the span of the galleries about 12 feet (7 cubits), and the height of the top of the arch 15 feet. The arches are four bricks thick, and were built without centring. The foot of the wall is sunk in a slight trench, and

the lowest course projects a couple of inches. For 78 inches high the building is of headers and stretchers, the headers being on edge; above this to the base of the arch (9 feet 4 inches) the headers lie flat. The method by which the arch was thrown across without any wooden framework to support it, is still practised in Egypt a little further south. It may be seen, for instance, near El Kab, and the roofs, though not so good as those of the ancient builders, are the best made in modern Egypt. The bricks used in the ancient arches are thinner and flatter than wall-bricks, and are grooved on the side to give them a better grip of the mortar. When we observe a section where the roof has been broken away, we see that it consists of four arches. In each of these the bricks lie on their edge but with a slight and uniform slope. The arches do not spring at right angles from wall to wall, but have a well marked rake, and the four layers of the roof have not the same rake; the second and the fourth are at right angles to the first and third. This arrangement has evidently given great strength, and, but for one fatal weakness, the buildings would to this day be almost complete. The weakness has been in the holes left for air and light. These were at the top of the arch, and at intervals of 12 feet; they were not large, certainly not more than 13 inches square; if there was a lining of wood they were still less. But the wood would be soon taken away for fires, and then children and idlers would yield to the fascination of making a little hole larger; in those few chambers where part of the roof remains, one can still observe that the breaks and gaps in the roof and walls have generally started from these air-holes.

Now in order to understand how this complicated roof was built, let us first consider the lowest of the four layers of the arch, and suppose the upper three removed.

The chief difficulty would be to get the first arch across. This would be done at the gable end of the chamber. Here the sides were about 9 feet high and the end wall would rise in a semicircle above this level. In the corner one brick would be placed on its edge, one end on the side wall, one on the end wall. Next to this two bricks would be laid, their upper edges leaning slightly towards the corner. The next course would reach from end wall to side with three bricks. So, course by course, the arch would grow, the end wall being gradually covered to the top and down on the further side until at last one course would stretch from the end of one side wall to a point about 12 feet from the end of the other.

It will be seen that, as the bricks are right angled and not moulded to the curve of the arch, there will be a space between the upper corners of each pair of bricks when the lower corners are in contact. This space is by the modern builders filled with a pebble.

An arch of a single brick's thickness was not strong enough. Three other layers were placed over the first, and of these the second and fourth were started from the opposite corner to the first and third, so crossing them at an angle and securing much greater strength.

When the long series of chambers was thus covered over, a smooth roof to the whole building was secured by building up the spaces between the roofs, and then smoothing the surface with loads of broken pottery. The rough brick was coated inside with plaster 1½ inches thick, a plaster so tenacious that it has lasted as well as the brickwork; when it falls, it falls in large mat-like slabs. The face of the plaster was whitewashed. The floor of the chambers seemed to have been made of a similar plaster, but the grave-digging of later periods had destroyed most of it. The door jambs and lintels were probably of sandstone. In more than one case such stones were found in place, but chipped and built in upside down, and with their Ramesside inscription and the breaks in the stone heavily plastered over. They were probably the original stones thus re-used, perhaps under Rameses III, after the building had been allowed to fall into decay. The whole group of buildings was surrounded by a wall 11 feet thick with a batter of about 1 in 10 on the outer side. This also was plastered and white-washed. When all the brick constructions were thus painted white, and the stone walls brilliantly coloured, the temple must have had a very bright appearance.

11. The plan of the brick-chambers is shown in PL. I; the original walls are in dead black, restorations of Rameses III or Seti II in broken black, and the stone temple in open line; this last is mainly transferred from Lepsius. The general plan is clear. The whole enclosure is surrounded by a stout brick wall, the temple is shut off from the store-houses by another, and also by one of stone. The chambers are generally arranged in double rows, and entered from a gangway between them; but there is no symmetry between the two sides of the building. Two of the central passages were colonnades and in one of these (I, 7) were four basalt statues of Sekhet, with parts of several others. The thin walls which are seen in

[illegible] From one of the pillars [illegible] and between this and the wall [illegible] another chapel: in it were the [illegible] of Pl. XXII. A photograph of this chapel is in Pl. II, 6; it shows the two sandstone vessels like mortars, which may be some form of altar. Fragments of similar vessels were found in three cases. Into this court opens the original gateway from the temple; the other openings in this wall are probably all of late date. The short walls at right angles to this are side-walls of funerary chapels. Further to the south (at 118) is a niche approached by two steps in brickwork, perhaps the base of an altar. An altar of sandstone, 3 feet high, which has a cornice at the top, is seen at the end of the east to west colonnade. At two points in the E. wall of this colonnade were very curious remains, pairs of seated statues, life-size, with the upper part worn away; they are made of unbaked mud, and the surface is therefore much damaged.

12. The main objects of the Rameside period found in the chambers were the broken oil-, honey- and wine-jars, made of a hard drab ware. These were chiefly found in the group of galleries to the N.W. Inscriptions recording the date of the vintage [illegible] A [illegible] of these [illegible] is given in Pl. XX, 1-16. The clay [illegible] The wine-jars are often [illegible] and taper downwards. The [illegible] are [illegible] conical or of the shape of an inverted [illegible], and some (as 17, 18, 19, 20) are of a [illegible] and much more [illegible] clay, and are of the [illegible] of a [illegible] coat.

There were generally no division-walls in the galleries, except those which were clearly of later date. But in one (60) there was a long brick bench, 15 inches wide and high, and in two cases we found the ground plan of an oval brick enclosure about 8 feet long and placed in the middle of a room; it may have been a bin for corn. At the door of several of the chambers was found a rough circular limestone dish about 15 inches in diameter and 2 inches thick with two lugs. But these may belong to a later period. Coarse tables of offerings were found in similar positions. Among other objects probably of the XIXth dynasty were two bronze spears (Pl. XVIII) made of thin folded and beaten plate and perhaps not intended for serious fighting, a few scarabs, some fragments of inlaid glass and the stelae of Ra-mes, Nefer-hetep and Nekht-Min.

13. In a niche in one of the smaller rooms (52) a scene had been painted upon the plaster. It was in a bad state of decay, for insects had eaten out all the vegetable material from the plaster. Miss Pirie managed to pick up the faint traces of the drawing, and from her coloured copy the outline of Pl. XX is traced. On the right is a sloping hill in dull red with dots of a darker tint meant for pebbles. On it stands the facade of a tomb from which the Ka of the deceased has come forth, and is kneeling before the tree-goddess Hathor, while his Ba bows down with its head over a dark-red vessel. The man is dressed in a white semi-transparent robe, through which his body shows pink. The goddess has a red skirt and white sash. She holds apparently offerings in one hand, and in the other a vase, red below, blue above, from which she is pouring upon the hands of the worshipper. The inscription above was illegible.

On the left side of the niche was a small male figure, not shown, kneeling with its face towards the goddess.

It may be that this, like the other funerary scenes, belongs to a later period than the XIXth dynasty.

Here may be mentioned the block of sandstone (PL. XXIX) inscribed with the name of Tuy the mother of Rameses II. It was found re-used as a threshold in one of the brick-chambers, and perhaps came from the stone temple.

14. Three fragments of tiles were found with the name of Sety II inlaid in blue on a white ground; one was at the north of the building, two at the south. The latter pair was accompanied by some trial-pieces from a sculptor's workshop, and by some ostraca written in a bold hieratic, unlike that of the wine-jars. The trial-pieces were rough tablets of limestone about 6 inches square, on which hieroglyphs and figures had been carved with varying skill. The first lesson appeared to be the *n* sign, the next a *neb*; the king's head in the war-helmet was another subject; too little space had been left by the pupil for the helmet, which was of half the proper height. With the first of the tiles, curiously, was an ushabti of Sety I, and fragments of these were found in two other places at low levels. It is not easy to see how they came there.

A piece of another tile of Sety II was in blue glaze, the inscription incised before glazing. It is of the same material and colour as a few small pieces, which were scattered in the southern galleries. These were models of headless oxen, about ¾ inch in length, and evidently came from foundation-deposits. Mr. Petrie has suggested that these are spare pieces made for Sety's funerary temple; the covered chambers of the Ramesseum would make a convenient workshop, for the temple of Sety is probably quite near.

15. By the door of one room (110) lay a sandstone lintel (PL. XIV). On one side it is inscribed, in very deep cutting, with the names of Rameses III; on the other side is painted on fine white plaster a scene of the bark of Osiris in its pavilion with Isis and Nebhat on either side. Only four colours, blue, red, yellow and a dull green, are used. Of this a coloured copy has been made.

CHAPTER IV.

XXIIND DYNASTY.

16. To this period of the XXIInd dynasty belong the greater part of the things found. Head-pieces from wooden coffins, scraps of cartonnage, mummy cloths, beads and ushabtis were the daily staple of finds, and whenever these could be dated with certainty it was to the XXIInd dynasty that they belonged. It seems that at this period the temple had fallen into disrepair, and was adopted as a cemetery by certain families of Theban priests related to the royal house.

Of tombs of this period more than two hundred were examined; three only, and these not rich ones, were intact. The walls of the funerary chapels remained in many cases; in three we found inscribed stone blocks (I, 87, 88, 161); but an untouched grave with its accompanying chapel we were not fortunate enough to discover.

17. An unrobbed burial of a man, Iuf-en-Amon, was found in chamber 102 (PL. I). A small shaft had been sunk to the depth of 9 feet close to the E. wall; from it opened a small chamber just large enough to contain two coffins. These were shaped roughly to the body, and lay with their heads north. White ants had found their way into the tomb and had eaten all the interior of the wood, leaving but a thin outer skin. Their branching tunnels were everywhere, hanging down even from the roof like coarse lichen.

A wooden figure of one of the four genii stood at the head of the east body. A wooden hawk of the shape of the *akhom* sign, 8 inches long, and painted blue, was upon the other coffin, over the chest; with it but nearer the feet stood the hawk-headed genius, while the ape-headed figure lay by its side; the last was made of clay. A box of the rudest, unglazed clay ushabtis, each 2 inches long, lay at the head of the western body.

The E. coffin enclosed another, the head of which was carved in human shape with inlaid eyes of bone and steatite; neither coffin bore any inscription.

The body to the W. was enclosed in a cartonnage case, and two coffins beside the outer one. Down the centre of the innermost coffin ran a *Suten du hotep* formula, the end of which, with the name of the deceased, had been eaten away by ants. On the cartonnage his name could be made out—Iuf-en-Amon.

It is noticeable that two bodies are buried together, one with more care than the other. In the numerous shafts which had been almost entirely spoiled, and in which only a basketful of the wretched little ushabtis were left, we often noticed that these were of two kinds, one a little better than the other; for instance, while one set were glazed, the others were made of clay covered with a wash of paint, but not fired. If

[illegible]

10. The third shaft in the tomb of Nekht-ef-Mut (XVI, XVII). We had found a small well, which, at 6 feet below the surface, opened into two chambers. In the southern one lay two wooden coffins, four figures in wood, and one dummy canopic vase. This had apparently been robbed; but as the coffins lay on a bed of gravel, not on the hard desert, we cleared further down. The chamber became a well in which, 9 feet below, two more burials appeared. These lay side by side, nearly filling the base of the well, and the spaces between the coffins and the sides of the well were filled with a red cement. The coffins lay with the head to the north, and were so large and heavy that it was impossible to remove them in one piece. They must have been put together in the tomb, for the opening of the well was too small to admit them. Indeed, when the cement was picked away, we found a handful of the wooden pegs (Pl. XVII, 8), with which the joints were fastened, thrown behind the coffin-head. The four funereal gualí of wood covered with pitch (XVII, 6-9) stood to the W. of the E. coffin; to the N. was a small wooden stela, like those of Pl. XXI, but uninscribed. The burial to the W. was enclosed in a rough outer coffin of 1½-inch planks, covered with pitch. Inside this, and fixed in its place by cement poured into the vacant spaces, lay another coffin. On the centre of this had been an inscription incised and painted blue on a plain wood ground. Inside lay the mummy with no enclosing cartonnage, but wrapped in cloth, stained black by the excess of bitumen with which the mummification was performed. On the base of the inner coffin the figure of Nut was drawn in yellow lines on a black ground. The other burial was that of Nekht-ef-Mut. On the outer coffin [illegible]

[illegible] The head of the coffin was painted, and the hands carved in wood and attached. They are crossed, the left holding a [illegible] sign ([illegible]), the right an [illegible] ([illegible]). This coffin was of wood, 2 inches thick. Inside it was the mummy, enclosed in cartonnage. The body was covered with very fine linen. [illegible] feet lay a little mummy figure, 8 inches long, made of bread and wrapped in cloth.

The decoration of the cartonnage was extremely bright; when first uncovered it really seemed as good as new, but a few days sufficed to remove the extreme freshness of the colour. The decoration is given in black outline in Pl. XVI, the undersides being shown in two detached strips. The face is gilt, the eyes are of inlaid shell, the beard of wood inlaid with blue glaze between lines of gilt. The wig is painted dark green with yellow stripes, the ground colour of the whole being white. The ends of the wig, the sun in the barks, the sun below Maat, and above the hawk on the breast, are all gilt. In yellow are the backgrounds of the columns of inscription; the wings of the hawk are dark green and the small inscriptions at the back are in black on white. This cartonnage is now in the Fitzwilliam Museum at Cambridge.

To remove the mummy, the back of the cartonnage had to be sawn off, for the material is very stiff and readily flakes. The method of construction must have been that the body after mummification was enclosed in a case of linen cartonnage, made on a model mummy, and this was laced together down the back. A piece of wood was laced on for the foot-piece, and then a layer of fine white plaster of about one-sixth of an inch was laid over the whole; this was moulded in relief for the figures, and on it all the decoration was painted. Between the cartonnage and the mummy the leather braces (Pl. XVII) lay upon the chest, with the stamped leather *menat* and its counterpoise, the *menat* bearing the name of Osorkon I. The mummy was very neatly bandaged; long strips about 6 inches wide were laid along the sides, and wider strips were wound round outside these. Under the outermost wrapping, and below the chin, was a score of beads made of a soft resin. Under the next bandage was the bouquet (XVII, 6); it is of grass stems on which have been threaded the corms of a Trichonema (identified by Prof. F. W. Oliver). Under this came a piece inscribed "*year* 3"; inside it was a piece of green linen, rather coarse, then a large white linen cloth covering the whole front of the body, and inscribed at the feet "*year* 33"; then came some fine muslin-like fabric followed by a lot of wrappings stuck together so as to form a rough cartonnage. On the thighs lay a flat sheet of papyrus written on both sides, which is, according to Dr. Spiegelberg, "a most valuable specimen of a text of the Book of the Dead of the XXIInd dynasty. The recto contains a chapter with the same title as chapter 162 of Lepsius' Totenbuch, but with different contents, then chapter 29 in extenso, and a great part of chapter 11 and 143. The verso contains chapter 17, lines 41–63."

The body itself had been soaked in bitumen, which had become much harder than the bones. Out of the bitumen near the neck was picked the necklace (XVII, 1) of small amulets in green glaze, blue frit, lapis lazuli, red glass and jasper. On the chest lay the scarab with silver wings (4), and, below this, the heart-scarab of hard stone, uninscribed. Two boxes of ushabtis, of the smallest and rudest kind, stood in the tomb, one at the head of Nekht-ef-Mut's coffin, the other on the left near the feet.

The fine wooden statuette (II, 4), inscribed on the base, "*priest of Amon in Thebes, Nekht-ef-Mut,*" was found in another chamber (I, 1), and doubtless does not represent the man whose tomb is described.

20. These were the only untouched tombs, but there must have been many much richer ones robbed, as the stelae and ushabtis show. Very many objects from these robbed graves of this period were recovered, found either in the shafts or in the earth near them. Planks from broken coffins were very common, and headpieces, some of them of rather good work (II, 9). Stamped leather braces (XVIII) were not rare; the stamped part is of yellow leather, with edges and back of red. They represent the king adoring Amon, and were all dated in the reign of Osorkon I.

A model sarcophagus (XVIII) in wood has a hawk upon the top, and is mounted on a sledge. In the only untouched burial in which such a hawk was found, it was placed within the outer coffin; but this was put together inside the tomb. Canopic vases (XIX) were repeatedly found in the wells, being left with the ushabtis when every trace of the coffin had been removed. They were generally of limestone, with a small cavity about 2 inches deep, empty and unused. But the dummy form—a solid block of stone—occurred several times. In one set, the lower in Pl. XIX, all but Amset are wrongly named.

All the canopic jars were empty except one set in pottery, which contained some organic matter soaked in pitch.

A few small wooden stelae were found of a type well known in museums (Pl. XX and II, 11). They generally represent the adoration of Hor-Akhti by a standing worshipper. These wooden tablets are about 1½ inches thick; they were covered with a thin layer of plaster, then painted, and in most cases varnished (2 and 14 are exceptions). The colours for the throne of Horus are always the same, the border being yellow, the ground of blue, with one quarter red. The throne stands sometimes (2, 11, 12) on a mat of green rush, with yellow cord crossties, and the mat lies on the desert (6, 12, 14).

Two of the tablets (13, 15) are of a different and much coarser style, and are apparently later in date.

21. Inscribed blocks of sandstone from the walls of funerary chapels were found in two spots. From one (Pl. I, 88 *b*) came the three pieces inscribed with the name Zed-mut-as-ankh, daughter of the 4th prophet of Amon, Nekht-ef-Mut (Pl. XXII). They lay upon the ground between the thick wall and the slight partition wall; with them were two rough tables of offerings, and two bowls or mortars of sandstone, 2½ feet high, 15 inches wide at the top, and with the sides about 2 inches thick (Pl. II, 6).

The background of the scenes is white; the coloured hieroglyphs are shown in line, those in solid blue or black are shown black in the plates. The dress of Zed-mut-as-ankh is a diaphanous white robe surmounted by a cape of some brown material, from which hang long, loose threads, not a fringe, but a kind of long nap over its whole surface. Linen of this kind has been picked up by Dr. Petrie from the great pit of royal mummies at Deir el Bahri.

The two pieces in Pl. XXIII, 2, 3, which show the collar of the high priest of Memphis, were also in this group (*cf.* Erman, Ae. Z., 1895, p. 23). Not far from these was another chapel (Pl. I, 87), from which came two other inscriptions on sandstone, the hieroglyphs in blue on a white ground (Pl. XXIII, 4, 5, 7, 8). Traces of colour remained on the brick walls; many chips of sandstone lay between them, and among them stood a large alabaster basin, or rather tub (Pl. II, 8), weighing about two hundredweight. On it was an incised inscription (Pl. XXVII, 8), showing

[illegible]

[illegible] doubtless stood upon the pedestal. The pedestal was inscribed upon the four sides with the name and titles of a fourth prophet of "Amon-Ra, King of the Gods," called Zed-Khonsu-ef-ankh. On each side of the altar stood (at *b* and *d*) one of the sandstone "mortars" seen in the photograph (I., 6). One of these also was inscribed with the name of Osiris in a cartouche. Some blocks of sandstone lay upon the floor. They were coloured red to imitate granite, and the inscription painted on it blue. Two stones (*c* and *d*) remained in position, and the rest could be fitted on to them. Thus *e* goes upon *d*, and *f* upon *c*. The two upper blocks are rounded above, and upon them must have stood the two blocks (*g* and *h*) of cornice. These are painted on blue, with red stripes outlined in black. There are traces of a procession of figures facing W. painted on the S. wall. Only those blocks which chanced to fall with the inscription downwards can now be read. The opening in the next wall W. of the great one is also lined with stone, and may be connected with this chapel.

The bold sketch of a Horus and uraeus pattern (XXIII, 1) is in red outline on uncoloured sandstone; it comes from another chapel (I, 26 to S.), and is probably a lintel.

The fragments of cartonnage formed a large though very uniform class of objects. The largest piece, a nearly complete case, is copied in PL. XXVIII and XXX*a*. The figures on it are painted in yellow, with red outlines, on a dull green ground; the hands are gilt.

Most of the fragments were quite small, and of interest chiefly for the names and genealogies that could be made out from them. They were generally decorated in red and green on a background of white, which had turned to yellow through the decay of the varnish. The most important pieces are copied in PL. XXIV and XXV.

[illegible] stone, and the game-base of a child. All were found near small robbed graves and are probably of the XXIInd dynasty.

No beads were found in the undisturbed burials, but great quantities of cylindrical blue glaze beads were scattered in the earth. In a few cases these were still partially strung into a network, small disc beads found with them serving to join the meshes. Flat scarabs of blue glaze, and figures of the four genii, made to be stitched on to the bead network, were also very common. There is not much variety in the beads; blue glaze and, rarely, blue frit are the materials, and the shapes are always the same.

23. The ushabtis formed the most numerous class of objects found. Of all kinds together there were several hundredweights, from the shapeless little mud figure 2 inches long, to the fairly moulded types in blue glaze 7 inches long, and clearly inscribed with the name and titles of the deceased.

All had been scattered by plunderers in the earth, few in the wells, most near the surface as if the boxes had always been handed up before being opened.

The ushabtis of one man were generally found in one gallery, but were sometimes scattered over two or three as if, when the tombs were rifled, the walls had been no higher than the spaces between them. Only the smallest and worst varieties were ever found in their boxes. The largest lots went so often very closely to two hundred that it is probable this was the ordinary number. Most are of the ordinary glaze, either blue or green, with the glaze above the inscription; others are of clay covered, after firing, with a wash of colour and inscribed afterwards; more rarely the name is written directly on the red clay, and in a few the clay is not baked at all. A rare form was moulded in cloth, the web of which is clearly visible on the glaze. Wood was used in three or four cases, but these may all have been of earlier date. The inscription is written in black or brown ink, except in one form where yellow paint is used on a blue background.

The names on the ushabtis with those from the

agments of cartonnage and wood coffins are given n PL. XXX, *a.*, and a specimen of each class is hown on PL. II, 11.

In a large group one observes that a few of the figures wear the short skirt or apron, while the rest are mummy-shaped. In one set, that of Nekht-ef-Mut, there were 10 of the first named out of 198. The proportion then is 1 in 10, and it may be that this was the usual ratio between overseers and workmen.

24. A little evidence was obtained as to the date of the use of iron. A long iron knife with a bronze handle lay on the floor of one chamber (32). Near it were many jar-seals and one pot, all of Ramesside times. Another knife of the same shape (turned up at the point) but all of iron, lay in the next chamber. It was below the floor level in an irregular shallow pit (40 inches deep) which had been dug in one corner of the chamber and lined with roofing bricks, and was therefore later than the first abandonment of the temple.

Another knife lay in a neighbouring chamber (36), and yet another in the S.E. part of the building. But all these places had been disturbed by robbers. As the knives were of one general type and were not found together, they probably belonged to one of the periods during which the whole building was in use, but whether that period was the XIXth or XXIInd dynasty cannot be determined. But bracelets of iron were found on two of the heaps of mummies of the XXIInd dynasty, or thereabouts, in chamber 33 (PL. I). From its use as an ornament we should expect that iron was then a novelty, and the position of the second knife mentioned suggests that it too is of the later period.

The iron axe (II, 7) is perhaps Roman. The wooden handle had been entirely eaten away and replaced by a mass of white ant tunnels, but the thongs of leather which bound it were untouched.

25. Of pottery there was curiously little, and, owing to the disturbances which had everywhere taken place, the dating was not easy.

The shapes 1, 2, 3, in PL. XII, were from the large XIIth dynasty tombs and are known as belonging to that period from other sites.

The group of small pots (4) is, from the foundation deposits, supposed to be of the XVIIIth dynasty.

The large jar (5) in hard yellow ware is the common wine- and oil-jar of the Ramesside period, while the long shape (7) in a dull red fabric, perhaps of the same time, often contains the masses of cloth, and of a white powder, which are so frequently found and are supposed to have been used in the preparation of mummies. No. 8 is, of course, of Greek period, like others found at Defenneh, and 10 is probably Roman.

To the XXIInd dynasty belong shapes 11 and 12 and perhaps 15. Nos. 16, 17, and 18, are the Coptic types, of which the decorated varieties were only found inside the stone temple.

A "pilgrim-bottle" in leather was found with a scratched pattern exactly like that of the same shape in pottery, suggesting a leather origin for this form.

26. A hoard of Ptolemaic bronze coins was found in a recess in the great north wall.

No. of specimens.	Reverse-Type.	Weights.	No. and weight in B. M. Cat.			Poole's Denomination and normal weight.	
		Grs.			Grs.		Grs.
2	Eagle l. on thunderbolt, wings open, looking back; between legs, E . . .	1580, 1485	Philadelphus,	158 .	1448	20	1340
2	Same type; no mark between legs .	1511, 1451	,,	159/63 .	,,	,,	,,
8	Eagle l. on thunderbolt; to l., cornucopiae; between legs, ℞	1164, 1153, 1123, 1105, 1103, 1099, 1093, 1031 . .	Euergetes,	87/8 .	1082	,,	,,
8	Eagle l. on thunderbolt; to l., cornucopiae bound with fillet; between legs, ΔΙ .	1178, 1130, 1089, 1040, 1036, 1002, 949, 891 . . .	,,	107/8 .	,,	,,	,,
5	Eagle l. on thunderbolt; to l., cornucopiae; between legs, ℞	602, 599, 558, 548, 523 .	,,	89/90 .	530	8	540
5	Eagle l. on thunderbolt; to l., cornucopiae bound with fillet; between legs, ΔΙ .	581, 548, 543, 539, 525 .	,,	109/10 .	,,	,,	,,
1	Eagle l. on thunderbolt, looking back; on l. wing cornucopiae; between legs, A .	706	Philopator,	35 .	711	10	670
13	Same type; between legs, E . .	805, 791, 789, 773, 742, 741, 722, 707, 697, 689, 689, 676, 645	,,	37/8 .	,,	,,	,,
11	Eagle l. on thunderbolt; to l., cornucopiae; between legs, ΞΕ	1193, 1174, 1166, 1154, 1134, 1123, 1106, 1105, 1093, 1078, 1057 . . .	Epiphanes,	71 .	1023	20	1340
13	Same type	611, 578, 570, 569, 569, 551, 547, 546, 543, 542, 541, 539, 534	,,	72 .	484	8	540

CHAPTER V.

TRANSLATIONS, ETC.

By W. Spiegelberg.

27. Pl. IV.—Fragments of the account of the battle of Ramessu II against the Cheta.—I give the fragments with references to the text published in L. D. III, 153: 1 = line 1–2; 2 = line 3–12; 3 = line 9–13; 4 = line 5–10; 5 = line 7; 6 = line 12. From this we see that there were two copies of the account of the Cheta battle. The fragments of scenes show the known Cheta types. No. 3, perhaps, represents some warriors advancing against the town under the protection of an enormous shield. (*Cf.* Wilkinson I, 242–243, for an attack under cover of a testudo).

28. Pl. VI.—Representations of the tomb of Sehetep-ab-Ra (XIIth dynasty).—In the upper register there are boats of the shape of the Middle Kingdom, tied together and accompanied by the commanders of "port" and "starboard." The inscription on the left is to be restored: "[Go] to the necropolis, make every effort, hurry to the West . . . in peace." The pilot at the prow is called "the follower Usertesen." In the lower register the ship is going by sail; on the right, the sacrifice of a bull is represented, while below, three men are carrying geese as offerings. It will be noticed that the name of the owner of the

Pl. VIII.—On the right hand the deceased was represented with a table of offerings before him. The inscription is to be restored.

"[An offering that the King gives to Tum] the chief of the great divine cycle in Heliopolis, that he may give [the sacrifice of bread and beer and] all good and pure [things] to the *Ka* of the devoted [to Osiris] Se-hetep-ab-Ra, the deceased, [son of] Mentuhetep, the devoted master."

A scribe introduces the three persons who follow. Of the two women, the first approaches the deceased "with the gifts of his districts (?) in the Delta, many in number," the second, "with the gifts of his districts (?) in Upper Egypt (?), many in number." The opposition of *tep-res* to *ta-meh* is rather interesting, and confirms to some extent Erman's view about the group *tep-res* (Aeg. Zeit., 1891, p. 119), though in our passage, *tep-res* means the whole of Upper Egypt as opposed to the Delta.

Whether the inscription "the scribe Rera . . ." belongs to an effaced figure, or indicates the place for a figure which was never executed, we do not know.

The group of half-effaced signs above the offerings of the gardener is not clear to me. The upper inscription contains the rest of the formula of offering.

Pl. IX.—The upper register represents the interesting scene of the human sacrifice, first interpreted by Maspéro. (*Cf.* the valuable remarks of Griffith in "The Tomb of Pa-heri," *ad. de loc.*, p. 20–21.)

The fragment of our scene can be restored from the tomb of Pa-heri (Pl. V). On the left the sarcophagus was represented on a sledge drawn by men and oxen. Then comes a man dragging with a rope the victim of the human sacrifice, the Teknu, wrapped up, as it seems, in an ox-skin. The Pa-heri scene is unlike this, in that the victim is there kneeling down. Then follows the scene known too by other representations (*v.* Griffith, l.c.), in which are represented two dancing buffoons, called *muu*. To them are addressed the words of the *neter sahu*: "Come, buffoons!" The long inscription continued in the second register has the usual exclamation: ". . . to the west in peace, in peace, to Osiris to the places of the Lords of Eternity."

Among the officiating persons there is mentioned the "chief reciter, Beba, son of Mentu-hetep, and the cup-bearer, Ubau Usertesen." The latter is giving incense before the mummy standing in a kiosk. Another cup-bearer, with the same name as the first-mentioned, carries a vase and a bowl with a rubber (?).

29. PL. X, stele 1 (beginning of XVIIIth dynasty).—The priest, Beba, and his wife, Hu-dadat, before "Osiris, the prince of the west, he gives life and distinction," and "Anubis, he gives distinction."

In the second register are represented two groups of persons whose connection with the above couple is not shown; on one side are the scribe, Ra-uben-nef, and his son, "the royal intimate," Ankh; on the other, a woman, called Aat-aba, with her children—two sons, Senseneb and Snu-aah, and two daughters, Atef-usar and Aah-hetep. I think that this genealogy will best interpret the very obscure statements of the stela. The formula of offering with the addition characteristic of the Middle Kingdom and the beginning of the XVIIIth dynasty, forms the contents of the three lines of inscription below.

Stele 2 (late period). A stela of offering in honour of a woman, Mut-ardas (Mutiritis).

Stele 3. (XIXth dynasty.) The chief of the workmen of the necropolis of Thebes, Nefer-hetep, standing on the divine bark of "Mut, the great mistress of Ashru." He is adored by two of his subordinates, both with the title, "*setem ash* of the necropolis of Thebes," who are represented with their families in the two registers below. Their genealogy is given here:—

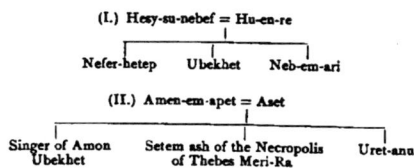

(I.) Hesy-su-nebef = Hu-en-re

Nefer-hetep Ubekhet Neb-em-ari

(II.) Amen-em-apet = Aset

Singer of Amon Ubekhet | Setem ash of the Necropolis of Thebes Meri-Ra | Uret-anu

Stele 4. (XIXth dynasty.) In the upper part are represented "Ptah, lord of truth, king of both lands, with beautiful face, who formed the gods, the great god, lord of eternity," and "Maat, daughter of Ra." Before them stands a dish with offerings, of which is said, "Pure, pure, for your *Ka* in all good things." The inscription underneath contains a prayer to Ptah and Maat:—

"Hail to Ptah, lord of truth, king of both lands, with beautiful [face], chief of his great place, master of destiny, who maintains fortune [for these expressions *v.* Maspéro, "Études égypt." I, 27], who gives life to both lands in (his) magazines (hmut). Adoration to Maat, daughter of Ra, mistress of heaven, [lady (hent)] of all gods, eye of Ra on his forehead, with beautiful face, in the bark of millions of years, mistress of the temple of Amon. May they give a good burial after old age (?) in the great West of Thebes, on the hill of Truth, for the Ka of the Osiris the scribe of Truth in the Theban necropolis Ra-mes, the justified."

30. PL. XI.—The first eight numbers contain brick-stamps. The brick No. 1 is stated by the inscription to belong to the Ramesseum, No. 2 bears the name of Rameses III, and No. 3 that of Rameses II in a curious form, known too in the temple of Bet-el-Walli. No. 4 gives the name of Amenophis IV, and shows that this king built in the western parts of Thebes, perhaps at his funeral temple, and probably in the beginning of his reign before the reformation, which took his interests far away from the old capital This building was not far from the Ramesseum, or its bricks would not have been re-used in that building. (For Amenophis' building in Eastern Thebes, see Wiedemann, Geschichte, p. 399, and Petrie, History, II, 223.)

The temples of Amenophis II (No 5) and Thutmosis IV (No 6), from which bricks were also obtained, were the next neighbours north and south. The name of Amenophis II with the designation *mery akhom* is not known to me elsewhere. There is in one passage (Rec. de travaux, 16/44) a similar name reading *mery Set*, and the conjecture may be allowed, considering the difficulty of reading these brick inscriptions, that Set is to be read instead of the hawk; 7 and 8 are from private monuments, probably tomb-buildings; the latter belonged to "the hereditary prince, the chief reciter in the good house (*i.e.* the tomb), the chief of the treasury *Dhuti Nefer*, the justified"; 7 gives probably the name of a certain *Nefer-au*.

31. For the jar-seals I refer to "Ostraca of the Ramesseum," where I have discussed the question more in detail. 9, 11, and 12, once sealed vases of *Bek* oil; 9 came from an oil plantation on Abydos in the Sety temple called "of happy heart;" 12

[illegible] the [illegible] for wine [illegible] 10, 13, 19 and 26, [illegible] of Abydos, [illegible] of the [illegible] of the [illegible] for the temple [illegible] "[illegible] of the [illegible]"

[illegible] they have on the top and the material is yellow clay, and generally have one or two impressions made, as it seems, with the finger. From this I think that the brackets 32 and 40 belong, too, to this series of seals; this would accord well with what is left of their inscriptions. The same type of seal is represented by 33, containing "honey of the Ramesseum"; whilst 35, "honey of the . . . ," is open, and of the cylindrical shape. A flat black shape is peculiar to 39, "honey of the house of Amon." Among the wine-sealings (19, 20, 23, 22, 28, 24, 27) there is to be noticed "wine of Thäre in the Delta" (19), "good, good, wine of the garden called Ka [of Egypt]" (20), "wine of the Ramesseum" (24), "wine of . . . of Rameses II" (23), "good, good wine of the Delta" (27). (*Cf.* Amarna XXI, 35.) Among the other fragments, there are some belonging probably to this series. So 25 may be restored with the help of a hieratic inscription "[wine of the garden of] Amon-Ra called] ashr [beloved]." 13 mentions the magazine of the Ramesseum, perhaps that of which the ruins still exist. 26 is perhaps to be translated "all things of the *Urat-Ashu*"; on 36 was mentioned a substance of the nursery garden: 18 is known by an Amarna sealing (Petrie, Tell el Amarna, XXI, 36), and 37 may be restored by Amarna XXI, 35. 17 is not known otherwise on jar-sealings; 38 mentions the king's jubilee; 39, 41, 42 and 44 bear the name of Rameses II; 43 gives the other name of the same king; 45 shows *Merneptah*, 46 Akhenaten (*cf.* Amarna XXI, 6), 48 Amenophis III, and 49 Thutmosis IV. The meaning and reading of the group in which Amenophis III occurs (47) is very obscure.

32. Pl. XIII.—2. Under the usurpation of Rameses II one of the names of Hat-shepsut is still visible.

3. Fragment of a stela giving only the name of a lady . . . *ari.*

4. (Dynasty XIX–XX.) Stela in remembrance of a man whose name has disappeared, perhaps belonging to the administration of the necropolis of Thebes. He was represented evidently in the upper register before some deities, among whom Min and Isis are still well preserved. Below stand the sons of the deceased, "the servant of the necropolis of Thebes Nekht-mut, Mer-ankh, Min-hotep, Amen-mena."

5. (Dynasty XXII–XXVI.) The variant for [illegible], which is not known before Dynasty XXIII, gives the terminus post quem. (*Cf.* L. D. 252, Sheshonq.) "Thou hast come in thy steps, thou hast passed thy body . . . the Osiris the god-beloved father (a title), opener of the two doors of the heaven in *Opet*, prophet of Amon-Ra in Opet, chief of . . . ."

6. Fragment of a religious scene.

33. Pl. XIV.—The bark of Osiris Sokar, called the *Henu* bark, is shown inside a wooden pavilion. Isis and Nephthys are on either side, each with three demons as "protection for the Osiris." The three-headed demon has the name "with the many faces." Over the whole scene is placed the winged disk of the Horus of Edfu.

34. Pl. XVI.—Cartonnage of "the god-beloved father, who opens the two doors of the heaven of Opet," named Nekht-ef-Mut, a splendid type of a cartonnage of the XXIInd dynasty. The representations must be studied in connection with the mass of material we now have for this period, in which this piece will take an important place. The texts covering the sides belong to chapter 125 of the Book of the Dead. The genealogy of this person, by other inscriptions here published, is ascertained as follows:—

I. Nes-pa-her-han
II. Za-khonsu
III. Meh-amen-hat
IV. Nes-par-neb
V. Nekht-ef-Mut

VI. King Har.sa.eset.meri.Amen

VII. Za.Mut.em.ankh — VIII. Har.sa.eset = IX. Aset-urt

X. Zed.mut.as [ankh] — XI. Ta.Khaemeth

35. Pl. XVII.—Leather straps of Osorkon I.

Pl. XVIII.—

1–4. Name of Osorkon I.

2. Osorkon I before [Khonsu] em [Uset] nefer-hetep.

3. Osorkon I before Amon.

4. Osorkon I before "Amon-Ra lord of heaven, king of the gods."

6. "The good god Thothmes I, justified by Osiris."

"The Osiris, royal wife Aah-mes living."

"The good god, lord of both lands Thothmes II, gifted with life, he has made it as his monument for his father."

So Aahmes survived her husband.

7. Thothmes III.

8. Sety II.

9. Perhaps Sebek-hetep II, [Ra-sekhem-s]uaz-taui.

PL. XIX.—Four canopic vases belonging to "the favourite minstrel of Amon-Ra in the fourth class *Nes-netret*, the justified, daughter of the prophet of Amon in Opet *Hor*, her * mother is *Ankhes-en-Aset*."

Four canopic jars with names of the four genii.

36. PL. XX.—A goddess (Hathor) in a tree (sycamore?) giving water and offerings to the deceased whose name is lost. He is kneeling before the goddess, behind him is the mountain of the west in which his tomb is seen. His soul is drinking the water in the shadow of the tree.

Nut is the goddess generally represented in a sycamore.

2. Stela (Dynasty XXII). "The singer of the harim of Amon, *Ta-sherat* .... daughter of the god-beloved scribe of the stable (?) of the house of Amon, *Nes-pa-neter*. . . ." She is adoring *Ra-Harmachis*.

3. Stela (Dynasty XXII). "The god-beloved *Bek-en-khonsu*, son of *Pe-da-mut* (Petemuthis), before *Ra-Harmachis*.

4. (Dynasty XXII.) "The wife and favourite *Zed-khonsu-as-ankh*, daughter of the prophet of Amon-ra-suten neteru (Amonra sonter), chief of the mysteries of the holy garments of the gods *Ser-Thuti*" before *Ra-Harmachis*.

5. The singer of Amon *Ze-Bastet-as-ankh* before the same god.

6. (Dynasty XXII–XXV.) The great prophet † of Amon in Opet, the one, splendid (?), true, the amanuensis of the house of Amon *Hor* son of *Pe-da-mut* offering to *Ra-Harmachis*.

PL. XXI. (Dynasty XXII–XXV.)—7. The divine father of Amon *Daf-ankh* before Ra.

8. (Dynasty XXII–XXV.) A woman called *Aset-uret* offering to *Ra-Harmachis* (Hor-akhti).

9. *Hor-akhti* (*Ra-Harmachis*) adored by a woman with the name characteristic of the Libyan period *Ka-ra-ma*.

Her genealogy is the following:

Mer-khonsu (prophet of Amon)
|
Har-sa-aset (with his father's title) Har Kheb
| |
Ka-ra-ma = Ser Thuti
("The god-beloved, the Wekil of the house of Amon")

10. (Dynasty XXII–XXV.) *Hor-akhti* worshipped by "the favourite and singer of Amon-Ra of the fourth class *Ta-da-ta-neb-henen*, daughter of the prophet of Amon-Ra, king of the gods (Amonra Sonter.")

11. (Dynasty XXII–XXV.) "The Osiris, the god-beloved, who opens the two doors of heaven in Opet *Min* . . ." offering to *Hor-akhti*.

12. (Dynasty XXII–XXV.) *Hor-akhti* worshipped by a woman called *Ta-da-aset* (?) *uret*.

13. (Dynasty XXII–XXV.) The woman adoring Osiris and the four genii of death (Amset, Hapi, Dua-mutf and Kebeh-senuf) has the following genealogy—

Kharu-shera (Coptic Khelshire) = *Shep-en-un*
(Divine father of Amon) |
Anutha
(Singer of the harim of Amon)

She is praying that heaven may be opened to her as well as "a house on the good way of the other world," that she may "go out and enter with Ra."

14. (Dynasty XXII–XXV.) A woman making an offering to Hor-akhti. Her name is lost, but the name of the father, "the prophet of Amon-Ra *Ankh-Khonsu*," and the grandfather, "the prophet of Amon-Ra, king of the gods," is still to be seen.

15. (Dynasty XXII–XXV.) The inscription of this tablet contains the well-known formula of offering of "the divine father of Amon," *Arti-er-tha*, whose father was a prophet, and whose mother was called *Zed-Hathor*. . . . He is represented in adoration before Osiris and Isis, who are followed by the four genii of the dead. A short general consideration of this beautiful class of wooden stelae may follow here. The origin of the stela from the false door of the tomb is now well known, though it had already begun to be forgotten during the Middle Kingdom, and some transition forms appear even at the end of the Old Empire. In the Middle Kingdom we can see in a good number of stelae an image of the tomb in which they stood; they were, so to say, the double of the tomb as the statue was that of the mummy. This conception is shown too by the custom at this period of dedicating a stela in the temple of Osiris at Abydos. In this way the deceased, though buried in his native town, marked his ideal tomb, the double of his real tomb, by the stela near the holy town of Osiris.

Now there was an old Egyptian habit of seeing in every building—palace, temple, or tomb—an image of the world, and it was by this idea that the decoration of many buildings was determined (*v.* Steindorff Baedeker, Aegypten, p. clxii.). So, when we re-

* All the texts have "his," which would make *Ankhes-en-Aset* mother of *Hor*. But the usual genealogic formula justifies the above conjecture.

† This title mentioned also elsewhere, *e.g.*, Mariette, Abydos, II, 21.

member that the stela was an image of the tomb, we are not astonished that it should show decorative elements that are common in the tomb itself. Even in the Middle Kingdom we find the sky or two skies as decorative elements on the top of the stela, corresponding to the sky represented in the tombs. In this way too is to be understood the winged solar disk so often represented upon the stelae. These cosmic decorations are found too in our series of wooden tablets. All except 13 and 15 show the heavens, 3–6, 9–12 with the winged disk, 8 and 14 without wings. No. 7 shows the heavens only. They are sustained in 4, 6, 8, 12, by the symbols of East and West, and in two others (3, 11) by the *Uas* sceptre, while in four cases (2, 5, 9, 10) it appears without supports. In 7 these look like a ladder. In 5, 6 and 12 the earth is indicated below, just as in the temples the floor decorations refer to the earth.

In 13 and 15 the decorative elements are somewhat indistinct, and this is one reason for dating them later than the other pieces.

The fineness of the drawing in some of them is of an inexpressible charm which can only be well felt before the originals.

37. Plate XXII.—Fragments of the tomb of "the fourth prophet of Amonra, king of the gods . . ., the royal treasurer, the only one friend, the chief of the treasury of the two lands, the eyes of the King of Upper Egypt, the ears of the King of Lower Egypt, Nekhtef-mut."

The legend above Isis is rather curious: "Isis the divine mother is given with thee, the sister of Osiris, who smites thy foes every day, when thou risest with (?) the solar disk! . . . . the soul is beside Sokar as the goose beside the ibis," etc.

2. A priest before a lady whose name has been destroyed. She was a daughter of the "fourth prophet of Amonrasonter *Nekhtef-mut*."

3. Four divinities upon a bark. In the lower register "Hathor, mistress of the necropolis," makes a libation (*nini*) before *Ze-mut-aus-ânkh*, a daughter of *Nekhtef-mut*, and says, "O, honoured by her town, the western gods are content with thee, thy distinctions are with *the counter of gifts* (name of a demon)."

On the other side a bark is represented, containing probably the shrine of a deity.

38. Plate XXIII.—All these fragments belong probably to the tomb of *Nekht-ef-mut*. To this personage refer the inscriptions 4, 5, 7, 8, the fragmentary state of which only allows us to state, that they mention the good condition of the deceased in the other world. For the genealogy see

6. "The scribe Anen, son of the *sab Anen*" from the tomb of *Anna*.

PL. XXIV.—All fragments of XXII–XXIIIrd dynasty.—2. belongs to a person named *Nekht-ef-Mut*, son of *Ze-khonsu-af-ankh*, who is not identical with the *N.* whose genealogy is given above, but with the present piece should probably be put the fine wooden statuette II, 4. In our cartonnage the traces of "Thebes" are still visible.

4. The woman *Ta-khnemeth* is said to be the daughter of a son of *Nekht-ef-Mut*, and of a royal daughter of the King Har-sa-aset *meri-amen* (Harsiesis). If we consider, that according to the inscription XXV, 3, *Ast-uret* is the daughter of the King *Harsiesis*, and the wife of *Harsiesis*, son of *Nekht-ef-Mut*, it is evident that the two fragments supplement one another, and that *Ta-khnemeth* and *Zed-Mut-as-*[*ankh*] were sisters.

39. PL. XXV.—1. Fragments of cartonnage belonging to a "son of the god-beloved opener of the two gates of the heavens in Opet, priest of . . . *Pa-my*, son of the prophet. . . ."

2. A lady, "surnamed *Aka*, daughter of a prophet of Amon-Ra, king of the gods."

3. contains the following genealogy:—

Nekht-ef-Mut King *Har-sa-aset-meri-Amen*
| |
Har-sa-aset = *Aset-uret*
|
Zed-mut-as-[*ankh*]

4. Cartonnage with name of "the divine father of Amon-Ra, king of the gods, *Zed-Khonsu-af-ankh*."

5. Cartonnage of the "only one friend, scribe of royal letters, *Neb-nteru* son of the prophet of Amon in Opet, the governor of Thebes, the judge in *Nekhen*, the *Sem* official, ordering the *Shendots*, prophet of *Maat*, daughter of Ra, *Nesi-amen*."

7. Fragments of cartonnage with the following genealogy:—

Bek-en-Khonsu
|
Ze-Khonsu-af-ankh
|
Har-sa-aset

8. Fragment of cartonnage with the name *Har-nekht*.

10, 11. Cartonnage with the following genealogy:—

Pe-da-Khonsu-uthes-kha and *Aith*
| |
Zed-Mut-as-ankh *Khonsu-maa*

Too fragmentary to show connections.

12. Cartonnage with three names, "priest of Amon *Neb enteru*, son of the prophet of Amon *Basa* and the god-beloved *Har-cheb*.

13. A lady, *Pe-da-amen-nesut-taui*, whose mother was *Shep-aset*.

14. Cartonnage with name of "the singer of Amon, minstrel of Amon-Ra *Mat*." On the same piece is mentioned a woman *Her-ab*.

15. Fragment with this genealogy:—

Zed-Khonsu
|
Nes-paut-taui
|
Har-sa-aset

On the edge is the name of a *hes* (?) *neter* named *Nes-pa-her* (?)

16. Fragment of cartonnage with this genealogy:—

Nes-paut-taui (Greek Spotus)
|
Har-sa-aset
|
Nes-paut-taui

The last was "divine father of Amon." His father and grandfather were "beloved of the god, opener of the two gates of heaven in Opet." The piece XXVI, 8, should be placed here.

17. This fragment mentions a "protection" ceremony for a lady called *Gat-Seshne*. (For the full text see Lieblein, 2544.)

18. *Zed-Bastet-af-ankh*.

19–22. Fragment of the cartonnage of "the god-beloved *Ary*," whose surname was Har-Kheb.

23. Cartonnage of [a priest of Amon-Ra] king of the gods, chief of the nurses of *Khonsu-pa-khred* (*Khonsu* the child) called *Ankh-pa-khred*, son of *Pa-shed-Mut*, who bore the titles of his father.

24. Fragment of cartonnage with the name of "a singer of the harîm of Amon, *Nes-khonsu-pa-khred*."

25. Two persons, *Zed-thuti-af-ankh* and *Nekht-ef-Mut*, are named; neither titles nor parentage can now be recognised.

PL. XXVI.—1. Fragment of a wooden coffin with the titles of a high-priest of *Khonsu-pe-ar-sekher-em-waset* whose name began with *Zed*.

2. Name of "the prophet of Amon in Opet called *Ankh-theker*." Perhaps this name means "Takeloth is living" and gives the date of the fragment.

3. Name of a priest or official at the "house of Ka-mephis" (*i.e.* Amon) named *Nes-ka-shuti*.

4. "The god-beloved father . . . Menkhet-Amen."

5. In its present state this only gives the names *Nekht-Bastet-eru*, a mother, *Amen-mes* and *Nes-pa-ka-shuti*. It is doubtful if this last name is identical with that of No. 3.

6. is treated in connection with XXVII, 7.

7. A man named " . . . *Uaset-neb-enteru*, son of *Amen-mes*."

8. See XXV, 16.

9. Fragment of cartonnage with the name " . . . *Auf-ankh*, son of *Har-sa-aset*." It is doubtful whether the passage of the inscription "Thoth comes to thee (fem.)" allows us to assume that the coffin was that of a woman.

The inscription on the limestone block gives the name of those for whose *Ka*'s the lost prayer was said. The two on the left mention a king's scribe *Pen-ta-uret*, and his sister and wife the singer of Amon *Ta-uret-her-ab-ta*, while the third gives three of his sons *Amen-nekht*, *Amen-hetep* and *Mes* . . . .

The inscriptions on the other side were in honour of a royal scribe and official of the necropolis of Thebes, *Amen-nekht-em-taui*, and his sister and wife the singer of Amon, *Ta-uret-em-heb*.

40. PL. XXVII.—1. (Dyn. XVIII.) "An offering that the king gives to Amon of Karnak the lord . . . that he may give thousands of all good and pure things that come on his altar on every festival that is in this temple, and a fair breeze coming from the *Khent* (north ?) to the *Ka* of the hereditary prince, the follower of the king since his birth, the great friend of the lord of both lands *Pa-ra*." This personage in the side inscription is named "chief of the south lands."

The statue, at the base of which runs the above inscription, stood in a temple, perhaps one of the funerary temples in the neighbourhood of the Ramesseum.

2. (Dyn. XIX.) This stela was rather difficult to read. It was never finished, for much of the inscription has not been engraved, but merely sketched in with black ink. These passages are shown in outline in the facsimile.

In the upper part of the stela are represented "*Unet*, lady of heaven, mistress of all lands, and *Sebek-Ra*, lord of *Het*."

Unet is a form of *Sekhmet*. The text gives a goddess *Āunt*, but there is no doubt about the reading *Unet*, for the correct writing is given in the corresponding inscription of the right side.

To both deities a prayer is addressed that they

[illegible]

[illegible] daughter of her daughter, *Tabens* (?), the daughter of her daughter, *Nehem*, the daughter of her daughter, *Rahsenet* (?), the daughter of [her daughter] . . . One figure with its titles is nearly effaced.

The last woman seems to have held some office at a temple of Isis. It will be noticed that there is one name over the sculptor having forgotten to put in the figure.

The men in the lower register are the following: "The administrator (*rudu*) of the castle of Rameses II," *Pa-Maru*, "the chief of the stable," *Paaufer*, "the chief of the stable," *Min-em-hat*, "the chief of the stable," *Ky-ari*, "the administrator of the palace (of Rameses II)," *Nefer-hetep*, "the beekeeper (?) of Amon . . ." The name of the next person is lost; the last was named *Min-em-heb*.

3. (Dyn. XXII.) Fragment from the edge of a black basalt sarcophagus, perhaps from the tomb of a "great steward of a divine spouse (*Duat neter*)." It shows a demon whose name seems to be "opener of the way."

4. (Dyn. XIX.) "Osiris, the great god, lord of *Rastau*, prince of eternity, receives the offerings of the captain *Ray*."

5. (Beginning of XVIIIth Dyn.) "The royal son *Sa-pa-ar*" worshipped by "the confectioner (? *ahhuti*) *Amen-em-apet*." This name has been engraved over another, in which . . . *mer* formed one sign. For the prince *Sa-pa-ar*, see Petrie, History, II, 44.

6. A Syrian goddess on horseback, perhaps *Asit*, adored by a woman. *Cf.* Müller, Asien und Europa, 316. Dyn. XIX–XXII.

7. The ushabti box, with the beginning of chap. 6 of the Book of the Dead, belonged to "the singer of the harim of Amon," *Nehem-Bastet*, whose genealogy—

King *Takeloth*
|
Har-em-apet = *Shep-en-Sopdet*
|
Nehem-Bastet

[illegible] the deceased, royal son of the lord of [illegible] Osorkon II." The father of *Shed-en-*[illegible] is known to us otherwise (*cf.* Lepsius, Königsbuch, 590).

41. Pl. XXVIII.—Cartonnage of the prophet of Amon-Ra, king of the gods, *Har*, son of the governor of Thebes, named *Aáa*. The register here reproduced relates to the judgment in the nether world, as does the long inscription of Pl. XVI, which covers the whole coffin, and contains chapter 125.

42. Pl. XXIX.—1. Slab, with an inscription mentioning the dedication of a monument by Rameses II to his mother, *Tuy*.

2. Osiris Sokar in his mysterious chamber, probably from the tomb of "the god-beloved father, chief of the workshops of the temple of Amon, *Zed-Thuti-a*[*uf*]-*ankh*, deceased."

43. Pl. XXX.—1. This is of the Middle Kingdom, and belonged to the *Sab ari Nekhen* (*i.e.*, a judicial title) *Har-hetep*. There is a great difficulty about the first sign. Is it *ankh*, or the still uncertain title of the treasurer, or *Khetem* (seal)? This would go very well with the common use of scarabs as seals, but as I do not know any other instance of this sign in scarabs, I think the title preferable to the other possibilities. Among the scarabs there is naturally no lack of those with the name of Thothmes III, though, as we know, they were not all made in his reign. The Nos. 4–6, 8–10, 12–18, belong to him, perhaps also the defective 7. No. 17 has the addition, "lasting by monuments in the temple of Amon"; 2 and 3 have the names of Amenophis III and his wife *Tyi*. Rameses II is represented by 19, and Rameses IV by 23 and 24. Among the other mostly decorative pieces I would notice only 45 with the inscription, "life is with me." This was evidently an amulet.

44. Pl. XXXa.—1. This chapter 125 (confession and epilogue) is not very different from the type of the Theban and Saitic period. Some orthographic variant will be noticed by comparing the different texts together. But as a type of the Dyn. XXII, the text is not without value for future studies.

2. This person is the well-known son of Sheshonk I, the high priest of Amon, *Aupuat* (Lepsius, Königsbuch, No. 569).

3. The fragment of this stele belonged to "the Osiris the fourth [prophet of Amen-em]-apet, the *sem* priest of [Sokaris?] *Nekhtef-Mut* . . . [his father is . . .] *auf-ānkh*, his mother, *Nes-Khensu-pe-Khred*. daughter of the governor of town (?) *Aputh*, royal son of the Lord of both lands, *Sheshonk I*, gifted with life."

This gives the following genealogy :—

```
                  Sheshonk I
                      |
                    Aputh
                      |
... auf-ankh = Nes-khensu-pe-khred
           |
      Nekhtef-Mut
```

4. Feldspar amulet, with a magic text belonging to a "chief of the goldsmiths of Amon."

5. Fragment of inscription in the style of the Middle Kingdom.

THE TOMB OF PTAH-HETEP.

BY

F. LL. GRIFFITH, M.A., F.S.A.

45. When Mr. Quibell, at the suggestion of Professor Petrie, asked me to undertake the description of these beautiful plates of the tomb of Ptah-hetep, the proposal was too attractive to be declined, although the time allowed was short and much other work was waiting to be done. The reflection has often been forced upon me how inadequately I was prepared for so important a task undertaken at so short a notice. I had never seen the tomb of Ptah-hetep, and no plan of it is anywhere to be found; information at first hand has, however, been placed at my disposal by Miss A. Pirie and Miss R. F. E. Paget, to whose devoted labours this full copy of the sculptures is due. Moreover, the publication by Dümichen of the greater portion of the tomb, with the essay of his collaborator Robert Hartmann on the zoology, has considerably lightened the work of a second editor, and the unskilled reader can here look for at least a summary explanation of the interesting scenes, though many of the details are left unnoticed. The plates were already printed off when copies came to my hands, so that the few corrections which have subsequently proved desirable can only be indicated in the letterpress.

This tomb was discovered in the course of Mariette's excavations commenced in 1850. The first reference to it is contained in E. de Rougé's important *Mémoire sur les six premières dynasties de Manetho*, p. 99. He mentions "le tombeau de Ptah-hetep, sorti des fouilles de Sakkareh," its identity with the present one among several tombs for persons of the same name being established by references to Ptah-hetep's priesthood of the pyramids of Ne-user-ra, and Men-kau-her. De Rougé's book was the result of his mission to Egypt in the winter of 1863–4.

The map of Saqqara in Baedeker's *Aegypten* marks this tomb just south of Mariette's house. It is strange that there is no reference to it in Mariette's *Mastabas*, no plan of it has been published, and the only general description of the tomb is contained in the following words of Mariette (*Voyage*, p. 41): "Il n'offre pas d'autre disposition que le tombeau de Ti, et on y trouve, comme partout, un massif rectangulaire qui est à proprement parler le mastaba, une chambre qui fait office de chapelle, un serdab, un puits, et enfin le caveau souterrain." From this it is evident that the tomb was a mastaba of the usual type, but the only part now accessible is the "funerary chapel" of Mariette's description. This is a single chamber with its entrance to the north; its relation to the rest of the mastaba is quite uncertain.

The chamber is rectangular. To judge from the plates the side walls must measure about 17½ feet, the front and back walls about 7½ feet. The entrance at one end of the north wall is about 3 feet 4 inches wide. The ceiling is sculptured to represent palm beams laid transversely, and the whole surface of the walls above a certain height is sculptured in low relief, two "false doors" in the west wall, however, projecting considerably. It is evident that when first discovered the sculptures were still exquisitely coloured; unfortunately the laxity and neglect of the administration in allowing travellers to take casts and wet squeezes has irretrievably robbed us of half the beauty and interest of the tomb. Only traces of colour now remain except upon one of the false doors, which is painted only and not in relief at all. Happily the reliefs have not suffered from the attacks which have proved so fatal to the painting. Although we can no longer admire the brilliancy of the colouring, which would have afforded such important aid in determining the nature of objects here represented, we can still wonder at the truth and delicacy of the outlines which the ancient sculptor wrought in the fine limestone of Turrah.

46. As indicated above, the tomb is not here published for the first time. First, in 1865, de Rougé, in the memoir already quoted, identified from its inscriptions the name of the pyramid of Men-kau-her;

[illegible] Dümichen's [illegible] in the autumn of 1869, the results of which are published in [illegible] volume, under the title of *Resultate der* [illegible] *Expedition*, the first consisting of lithographed plates, including amongst other things the greater part of the sculptures in this tomb and the second of photographs in which I have also been able to trace two which comprise at least one view (pl. xiii) from the interior of the tomb. It is from Dümichen's copies that the scenes from the tomb have become widely known through reproductions in the works of Maspero and elsewhere. The publication is more accurate and complete than was then usual in works of Egyptology, and it preserves the record of several details now destroyed; but the present copy is in almost every particular far superior to it. Hartmann's appendix of notes on the zoology, though tending to far too much differentiation of species, is often suggestive.

In or about 1878, Mariette, in his *Voyage dans la Haute Égypte*, pl. xi, gave a photograph of the fishing scene on the east wall, and Perrot and Chipiez (*Histoire de l'Art dans l'antiquité*, Tome I, 1882) give an interesting sketch of the west wall with the two doors in Fig. 115, and details of the painted door in their pls. xiii, xiv, all from copies by Bourgoin. There are also several casts in existence, a set being in the Berlin Museum.

47. In the autumn of 1895 application was made to the administration of antiquities for permission to copy the sculptures, and by the kindness of MM. J. de Morgan and E. Brugsch Bey the entrance of the sculptured chamber was cleared and Mariette's house was put at the disposal of Miss Pirie and Miss Paget, who worked at the copying during the greater part of December and the following January. The present plates are reduced from their careful tracings, with the exception of Pl. XL, which is only a rough sketch.

As usual, the general movement of the scenes is from the exterior to the interior, while the large figures of Ptah-hetep seem to gaze upon them, looking outwards. The scenes begin at the sides of the doorway in the thickness of the wall (Pl. XXXVII), where priests and servants are bringing offerings. Within the chamber active occupations of the deceased are represented on the east wall; ritual and the ceremonial supply of food on the west. On the north wall, west of the entrance (Pl. XXXVI), is the slaughter of oxen, and the conveyance of supplies for the table of offerings on the west wall; but above these scenes and continuing over the door (Pl. XXXV, lower half) is a distinct scene belonging to the series on the east side, and representing Ptah-hetep at his morning occupations, receiving reports, etc., while servants attend to his toilet.

The east wall (Pls. XXXI–XXXIII) is occupied by two scenes, in each of which is a large figure of Ptah-hetep. In the first scene (XXXII and lower half of Pl. XXXIII) he is looking on at sports, vintage, hunting, boat-building, fishing and boating scenes—"amusements" as these are called in the inscription. In the second (Pl. XXXI and upper half of Pl. XXXIII) he is, later in the day, receiving his dues from the cattle and poultry farmers, and from the huntsmen.

The south wall (Pl. XXXIV and upper part of Pl. XXXV) is occupied by rows of friends and servants, some of the latter representing the estates of Ptah-hetep bringing supplies for his table, etc. This apparently completes the series of non-funerary scenes.

The west wall, towards the region of the dead, is occupied by the ceremonial scene of the table of offerings (Pls. XXXVIII and XLI) between two false doors of different patterns (Pls. XL and XXXIX). The meaning of this arrangement is not easy to apprehend, but from the figures and inscriptions on the southernmost (Pl. XXXIX), that would seem to be a magic portal through which Ptah-hetep might pass out into the scenes of earthly life and retire again from them. It is an outer door. Pl. XL shows a curtained and, probably, inner entrance; perhaps it is intended for that to the sepulchre itself, perhaps simply for that which shut off the kitchens and store-houses from the dining-hall, where the ceremonial repast of the deceased is served (Pls. XXXVIII, XLI). But to arrive at the real significance of such devices in tomb sculpture would require the study of a large number of contemporary and earlier examples on the spot.

We will now take the plates in such order as seems best for following the logical sequence of the scenes.

48. Pl. XXXVII.—*Sides of doorway.*—On each side the bringing of offerings is represented in four rows: on the left (Düm., *Res.* I, x.), oxen above, and miscellaneous offerings below, are brought in by "*Ka*-servants"; on the opposite side the subject is much the same, but the top row is occupied by two sorts of geese, pintailed ducks (?), widgeon (?) (*sekhi*), teal (?) and pigeons. As the "*ka*-servants" figure so largely

in this place, it is best to consider these scenes as belonging to the furnishing of the tomb, and of the table of offerings shown on the west or right-hand wall; but they are evidently preliminary and not very important.

The real business commences inside the chamber. Here, on the north wall, are two sets of scenes, as already stated, the movement of the lower one being towards the false door, while the upper scene, which is continued over the entrance, belongs to the daily life of the man as before death. It appears that the deceased was supposed mystically to continue his earthly occupations, so that these representations were intended to depict part of his life after death, rather than that they were simply meant for the contemplation of his *Ka* and of his kinsmen who visited the tomb in order to recall his former life on earth.

Non-funerary Scenes.

49. Pl. XXXV *lower half.—Upper part of north wall.* (Extracts in Düm., *Res.* I, x.)—Ptah-hetep, seated, with body-servants, officers of the estate, musicians, etc., in attendance. This scene apparently represents the great man at his morning avocations indoors, reading and hearing reports during the progress of his toilet. One man is attending to his feet, and another to placing his wig; another brings linen; another advances from behind, carrying a box on a stand, perhaps containing toilet ornaments; and below him a fifth attendant is holding in leash three hounds and a monkey. In the two middle rows his twelve officers face him, kneeling each on one knee; one of them hands him a written document. Above and below, *i.e.* on either hand, are musicians, two harpists, one flute-player, one clapping hands, and another snapping his fingers. On the extreme right are four dwarfs looking over their master's jewelled collars and other ornaments. To the left of Ptah-hetep a favoured person is helping himself from an abundant pile of provisions; he is the chief stone-mason Sethef, doubtless the builder of the tomb.

It is probable enough that, as in other scenes, the artist has here crowded together a number of occupations, which need not be supposed to have all been going on simultaneously.

50. Pl. XXXII and lower part of Pl. XXXIII.—*North end of east wall.* (Düm. *Res.* I, viii.)—Ptah-hetep looks on at vintage scenes, sports, hunting, fowling, etc. The inscription over his figure reads: "Seeing every pleasant amusement that is performed in the whole land," and concludes with the titles and name of Ptah-hetep (see pp. 33–4). The figure is life-size; the necklace, with four large beads and a pendant, is unusual. He is accompanied by the "*sab-ad-mer*, Seshem-ka," and a little boy who is "his elder son, whom he loves, the *sab-ad-mer*, Ptah-hetep." The boy holds a captive hoopoe by the wings. The scenes are arranged in seven main rows, the topmost three of which are in Pl. XXXIII, and are as follows:—

In the left-hand top corner the subject is now damaged (see Düm.); it is the usual one of taking the cattle across the water; to the right of this, men are gathering papyrus and carrying it away in bundles.

Second row.—The boys' games here represented are very remarkable. The first three groups on the right are, unfortunately, injured now, but are complete in Dümichen's copy. The game of throwing pointed sticks is found also at Beni Hasan (*B. H.* II, pl. vii). Behind the stick-throwers are two boys seated in a difficult position, holding their feet in their hands; and below these a boy is carrying on his back two small children, who, by holding each other's legs, form, as it were, panniers on each side of him: he is evidently playing donkey. Behind these, two boys are standing together, each with an arm round the other's neck, and holding the arm of his fellow with the other hand; they appear to be going in opposite directions, and each, perhaps, is endeavouring to free his own arm, and get the other's head in chancery. Next is a youth wearing a kind of shoulder scarf, who is striding towards two lads sitting on the ground, each of whom has the heel of one foot resting on the toes of the other below, his hands placed also one above the other, and with fingers extended. The accompanying inscription seems to read, "female calf on the ground." Next we have a boy on all-fours upon the shoulders of three of his companions, and behind this group six boys appear to have formed a ring, and then, putting their feet together, and falling back at full stretch, to be making a revolving circle on their heels: the inscription says, "go round four times." In the last group, a boy, kneeling on the ground, is trying to catch the feet of his four companions, who confuse him by simultaneous attacks on all sides. The inscription may be read, "Behold, you have kicked me (?). My sides are weary"; and, "I have caught you."

[illegible] through the flesh of the leg, and the juice is wrung out with great force by two persons, one of whom, in the [illegible] his whole body in doing [illegible] while the juice drains from the leg. At the end of the row a chief scribe named [illegible] stands in a characteristic attitude of [illegible] attention before the great man, probably receiving his commands.

These three rows seem to be in the nature of an addition to the four below them, which follow in the usual perspective order of high land to low land, *i.e.*, proceeding from desert scenes at the top to river-bank, marsh, and river scenes below.

Fourth row (PL. XXXIII).—Hunting in the desert. The hunting-dogs are all of the "type of the large and strong greyhound, called *slughi* in North Africa, with broad, pointed ears and curled-up tails" (Hartmann). They are distinguishable at once from the wild beasts by their collars. Taking the animals in the upper division in order from left to right, we have first, two hyaenas, or, perhaps, as Hartmann suggests, wild dogs of the desert, *kelb es semahh*, *Canis pictus* (?), one of which is caught by a slughi. Next, an oryx worried by a dog, then a gazelle suckling her little one, then an ibex caught by a dog, then two leopards and two jackals. Below, we have a huntsman, "the *ka*-servant, chief attendant Ara" (see DÜM.), comparatively well wrapped up against the cold night, and holding two hounds in leash. He is watching for a lion. A cow, with her calf, has been placed as a bait, and the lion, a short-maned male of the Sennaar type, has seized it by the muzzle, to its dire terror and distress. Next come a gazelle and an oryx, each captured by a hound. Lastly, we see the lyre-shaped horns of a bubale (?) behind two ox-like creatures, one of which is caught by a lasso or bola.

This last group should be of exceptional interest to zoologists who are disposed to assert that wild cattle do not, and probably never did, exist in North Africa. [illegible] is, in [illegible] picture [illegible] to represent [illegible] [illegible] confirms the impression conveyed [illegible] viz. that the animal in question [illegible]. The best proof of this is to be found [illegible] In *B. H.* I, pl. xiii, we see a similar animal figured in a desert hunt, represented in the [illegible] of Ameny. In the corresponding scene from the tomb of Khnemhotep, *B. H.* I, pl. xxx, we see [illegible] of these beasts shot by arrows, and the list of the hunting spoils is handed in to Khnemhotep by the scribe, Nefer-hetep. In this list, *l.c.*, pl. xxxviii, [illegible] lies our proof. It enumerates hyaenas (*hetet*), oryxes (*maheḍ*), wild cattle (*sma* or *smu*), common antelopes (*gahes*), ibex (*nau*), bubale (*shesau*), all of which are to be seen with the other animals in the desert scene, *l.c.*, pl. xxx. The Egyptians, therefore, wrote the name of the animal with a determinative of an ox, and this shows what they thought of its affinities. The same animals are beautifully and characteristically figured in *El Bersheh* I, pl. vii. Again, on a fine scarab of Amenhetep III, the photograph of which has been shown to me recently by Mr. Fraser, we have an account of the king's hunting a great herd of *sma* (with the determinative of an ox lowering its horns for attack) in the country of Sheta (?). Unfortunately, we do not know where this place was; probably it lay somewhere in the region of Mesopotamia, though it may have been in Nubia. We thus see the meaning of the name *sma-ur* (*sam-ur*), "Great Wild Bull," in the pyramid texts as an appellation of Osiris. The word *sma* means "slayer," alluding to the animal's fierceness and strength. Cf. also PRISSE "*Art*" II. 24, dyn. xviii; *Berl. Pap.* II. 206.

In the upper part of this row are a common gazelle lying down, an ichneumon or large rat, a jerboa running into its hole, and two hedgehogs, one of which has caught a grasshopper.

The plants as usual are quite unrecognisable in the quaintly simplified rendering of the ancient artist.

Fifth row.—Scenes on the river bank: cutting open fish to dry in the sun; "twisting ropes of boat-building." In the boat-building scenes, where the men are occupied in binding together the bundles of papyrus stems of which the boats were formed, one man, whose young son is taking care that he does not slip as he tugs, says: "Kindly protect these things for me," or, perhaps, "Kindly help me in this." Another says: "O strong lad, bring me ropes!" and the boy hands him two coils with the words: "O father, here is this rope for thee." The excellent supply of food for these men is represented above them.

Sixth row.—Fowling. Two clap-nets are closed, the one by six, and the other by seven men. The signal is given by the chief scribe, named Up-em-nefert. Over the six men, who are on their backs, is the inscription, "Fowling by signal" (?) or "by counting," *i.e.*, one, two, three, and away! in order that the tugs may be simultaneous; and below, "Pull, comrade, you have made a catch!" To the left two men are taking the birds (from the net?), and putting them in boxes or cages. One says, "Put these in this box." The other, "Behold, I am hesitating over a full box" (?). Behind them, "the superintendent of robes (?), Ahy," is running with two full cages on a yoke: "Run swiftly, thy occupation is in life" (?), followed by "the superintendent of robes (?), the ka-servant Aau," with one cageful of birds, and others captive. Immediately in front of Ptah-hetep, the steward, Senb, is presenting some of the spoil.

Seventh row.—Boating scene: a mock (?) combat between the crews. To the right of the boats a goose is brought to Ptah-hetep by "the chief scribe, *Seshem-nefer*, whose good name is Thefu." In the farthest boat to the left we may notice a partially bald old man eating in comfort, and enjoying the scene, a favoured friend of Ptah-hetep. He is entitled, *me-henk-f mer-f amakhu-f mer . . . . Ankh-n-Ptah*, "his beloved and trusty *mehenk*, the chief sculptor Ankh-en-Ptah." *Mehenk*, of uncertain meaning, is an appellation bestowed on architects or artists of the tombs: *cf.* ERMAN and SETHE, *A. Z.*, xxxi, 97. In any case, we have here the name of the really great artist who executed these reliefs, signed in the corner of his masterpiece.

51. PL. XXXI, and upper part of PL. XXXIII.—*South end of east wall.* (DÜM. *Res.* I, pl. ix.)—Ptah-hetep receiving the produce of his farms and huntsmen. The figure of Ptah-hetep is very similar to that in PL. XXXII, but here he is wearing a different wig and a false beard. He is not merely wandering over his lands to see how all is going on, but is acting in a definite official capacity. According to the inscription, he is "seeing the tribute, the contributions of the fortresses and cities of the south and north, and of the *wakf* (*per zet*)." Accompanying him is another "elder son" (*cf. B. H.* I, p. 43, for an "elder son" and a "second elder son"), Akhet-hetep, who, like his brother, Ptah-hetep, was also *sab-ad-mer*, which may be freely translated "inspector of canals," an important post in Egypt; he holds two little birds captive. In front of Ptah-hetep we have again seven rows of scenes.

Top row (PL. XXXIII).—Review of the corps of trained youth bringing in a prisoner. Six pairs of youths are wrestling; one has the name of Akhet-hetep, and may be Ptah-hetep's son of that name; another is called Thefu. In front, six youths are driving before them a prisoner; this important figure is here imperfectly represented: Dümichen's copy (pl. ix) shows the two arms of the prisoner tied together with cord above the elbow, as in the hieroglyph of the prisoner. Prof. Erman has kindly verified this figure on the cast at Berlin, which shows that Dümichen's version is correct. The figure in our plate is accurate so far as it goes, but the second forearm and hand, and the cord with which the arms are bound, have been overlooked, probably owing to the bad light in that corner of the tomb, for mistakes in this copy are singularly few. The inscription also reads, "Here comes a foreigner, O, hearken to his desire"; said ironically, no doubt.

This row evidently represents the military section of Ptah-hetep's people. Young soldiers were called *neferu*, "goodly youths," in the Old Kingdom, and *zamu*, "young men," in the Middle Kingdom, usually written with the determinative of youth. Evidently, boys were taken at a rather early age, and trained to military exercises. The prisoner resembles his captors exactly, but it seems clear that he is really a young soldier taken from a hostile band, and brought in triumph to Ptah-hetep as spoil of war.

Second row.—Contributions of the huntsmen. Four men,—one "the ka-servant, the *sab*, Ikyk, strong-of-voice," are dragging two sledges with strong cages upon them, one containing a lion, and the other a leopard. Behind these a man is carrying, by means of a yoke, a bubale, an ibex, a common gazelle, and an oryx, tightly bound together—an enormous load, to which yet other things are added—; but perhaps they are only heads and hides of the animals. He is followed by Ahy, with a gazelle over his shoulder, and afterwards comes the *sahu* Seshem-nefer carrying hedgehogs and hares in cages. Finally Khnem-hetep, in a huntsman's dress, leads his four *slughis*, and a smaller dog of a different sort, together with two hyaenas (or *Semakh* dogs), and a whelp (?), all of which seem quite tame, and are held by nothing but a leash; but perhaps this must not be pressed, as even leopards are so represented in some tombs. Hartmann considers the upper group to be of the [illegible] with an elegant antelope, rarely figured in the scenes. This last is identified by Hartmann as *Antilope Dama*; he also gives different names to all the other animals in the row, but the present copy confirms the impression that the first four represent simply examples with extra fine horns of the species of large antelope usually figured in the early scenes. Even the last may represent only the common gazelle, with its horns as seen from the front, but it must be admitted that such a style of drawing would be quite exceptional, and it is better to consider the animal as intended to be of a distinct species.

Fourth row.—Herdsmen, and scenes with cattle. Two cattle being fed or doctored. See also DÜM., pl. ix who has one or two more signs here, but their meaning is not clear. The "director of herdsmen" leans on his staff, another man faces him, and a third is kneeling at the feet of a fourth (a foot is just visible). A cow is calving, and a number of calves are tethered above (the last of these is on PL. XXXII).

Fifth row.—"The royal acquaintance, the superintendent of a cattle estate (?), Herbat," who wears a necklace, is leading some oxen. The inscription above reads: "Seeing the fat cattle, the tribute of the feast of Thoth (19th Thoth), from the fortresses and *Ka*-cities of the North and South, and (?) of the *waqf*-estate (*per set*)."

Sixth row.—The "superintendent of the granary, the *semer* of the steward, Ka-hap," stands respectfully before Ptah-hetep. Following the long-horned ox which is led behind him is "the superintendent of labourers, Kaach." The short-horned ox is driven by an aristocratic person, the "ruler of a fortress, Herkhu." The inscription above reads, "seeing the counting of oxen of the stalls of the fortresses and *ka*-cities of the *waqf*."

Seventh row.—The "superintendent of the corn store, the *semer* of the steward, Ka-hap," again leads. The inscription at the top runs: "seeing the homage, the fowl offered by the fortresses and *Ka*-cities of the North and South belonging to the *waqf*." First [illegible] Thus, in the upper division [illegible] of geese (probably [illegible] legs, and [illegible]) [illegible] in number [illegible] and [illegible] swans (very unusual, probably the [illegible]). Below these are [illegible] pin-tailed ducks [illegible] (widgeon?), [illegible] pigeons, and [illegible] birds that with their long legs should be the [illegible] of some gallinaceous bird, but very likely they were intended to represent quails or wild partridges in general. From comparison with a list of domestic birds in the Rhind Papyrus (*P. S. B. A.*, xvi, p. [illegible]) it seems clear that these are partridges or quail. The quail abounds in Egypt, and the eggs are found in enormous quantities by the fellahin when gathering their crops. Doubtless the eggs thus found were hatched by a foster-mother, or perhaps artificially, to provide delicate food for the table of the nobles; and the birds would scarcely be allowed to grow to full maturity, so that the chick-like representation of them when in the farmyard was characteristic.

52. PLS. XXXIV and upper part of XXXV.—*South wall.* (Extracts in DÜM., *Res.* I. xv.)—It is difficult to say whether these scenes should be connected with the funerary or with the non-funerary. The true funerary meal, with ritual, is shown on the west wall after the usual style, but here on the south wall also *ka*-servants are engaged and lectors are named.

In the top row (PL. XXXV) a vast pile of offerings is raised; in the second and third rows are female servants representing the estates of Ptah-hetep, with accompanying inscriptions giving the names of these estates, and, more important still, the nomes in which they were situated. The first two in each row are distinguished as royal residences, and the first of all in each are residences of the reigning king, Assa. In the second row we have (1) the residence of Assa, called S-ankh-Asp, in the XXIst nome of Upper Egypt, followed by (2) the residence of Khufu, called Tu (?) in the XXth. In the third row is (1) a residence of Assa called S-ankh-taxt, no doubt in Lower Egypt, followed by (12) a residence of Sahura called Mer-nefert, in the VIIth nome of Lower Egypt. The others follow these in fairly close geographical order viz:

Second row.—One (3) in the XXth nome of Upper Egypt (Heracleopolite), one (4) in the XXIst, one (5) in the XVIth (the Oryx). The rest appear to be in Lower Egypt, viz.: one (6) in the VIth (Kois, the "Wild Bull"), two (7, 8) in the VIIth nome (Metelis ?), and two (9, 10) destroyed.

Third row (PL. XXXIV), one destroyed.—One

(14) called the city of Osiris, in the IXth nome of Lower Egypt—Busiris—the sign for which is complete in Dümichen; then two more (15, 16) of which the nome signs are destroyed, one (17) in the IIIrd or Libyan nome, one (18) in the Xth Athribite, one (19) in the IInd or Letopolite, and lastly one (20) in the XIIth the Sebennyte.

The arrangement is interesting: it seems to follow from north to south and from west to east, first for Upper and then for Lower Egypt. Five nomes are given also with the estate-names in MAR., *Mast.* p. 383, and from these and other sources a fairly complete nome-list might be constructed for the Old Kingdom, differing in some respects from the nome-lists of the Ptolemaic time.

As to the estate-names, we may note that several have cartouches attached to them, which may refer to the granting of the estates by certain kings. In one case, 3, we have a name identical with that in 17, only it is in the XXth nome of Upper Egypt instead of in the IIIrd of Lower Egypt. This puts us on our guard against identifying with too much positiveness estate-names occurring in different tombs. It is, however, worth noting that 5 occurs in the extremely early tomb of Nefer-maat at Medum (PETRIE, *Medum*, pl. xix), perhaps in the time of Senefru. 16 is connected with Senefru, and the same name frequently occurs, *e.g.* in Merab's tomb (where it is attributed to the contemporary king, Khufu), in the tomb of Seshem-nefer I, in that of Ka-neferu, in that of Zaza-em-ankh of the beginning of the Vth dynasty, in that of Nenkheft-ka, in that of Seshem-nefer II, in that of Thy, and in that of Ptah-hetep II whom we believe to be the son of our Ptah-hetep. 20 also occurs in the tomb of Seshem-nefer II, in that of Pehenuka, and in that of Ptah-hetep II. 15 is found in the tomb of Seshem-nefer II, who probably died before the reign of Assa began, and 13 in that of Pehenu-ka, where it is attributed to the same king and should therefore be identical. 7 also occurs in the tomb of Seshem-nefer. Compare the interesting paper by Miss Murray in *P. S. B. A.* xvii, 240, in which most of the above references are given.

Fourth row.—Butchering scenes. Over these scenes are a number of short sentences which are as follows. Cutting off the haunch—"Pull hard!" "I will tug well." Over man with heart—"Come, man, [to] this heart!" Over man with foreleg—"Give me meat for the *ka*-prince!" Severing the foreleg—"Tug well!" "I am doing (so)."

Fifth row.—"Bringing offerings by the *ka*-servants of the chief next to the king, Ptah-hetep." From their titles these *ka*-servants are people of rank, including a canal inspector Ptah-hetep (apparently the son figured on PL. XXXII), a superintendent of the granary and his assistant, and a chief scribe.

SCENES CONNECTED WITH THE TABLE OF OFFERINGS.

53. PL. XXXVI.—*Lower part of north wall at side of door.* (DÜM., *Res.* I, xi.)—Preparing and bringing offerings.

Top row.—"Bringing things to the superintendent of the pyramid city, upper priest of the Nefer-pyramid of Assa, first below the King, Ptah-hetep, by the *ka*-servants of the wakf."

Second row.—"Bringing tribute, sprouting things and all good things by the *ka*-servants, etc."

Third row.—Over a man cutting off foreleg of an ox, evidently the finest of the slaughtered—"Let the divine servant and priest come to this foreleg," to which the second, at the hind leg, replies, "Behold I will carry off (to him) its haunch!" A man cutting off the foreleg of the next beast calls out to his neighbour, "Ho! pull me this," but the other, who is busy with the haunch of the last animal, replies, "I am attending to this" (lit. "I am making these to happen"). A fifth man, who is holding the haunch of the second ox, extends his hand to the "chief *uab*-priest of Pharaoh, the physician Akhetarna," saying, "See this blood!" The priest smells the blood on his hand and gives his verdict, "This is purity."

Fourth row.—Further cutting up of oxen. Taking the scenes from left to right the inscriptions run: "Pull hard!" "I am doing (so)." "Behold this heart." "Lift up, neighbour." "It is in my hand (?)." The man with the bowl says, "Give me this blood."

54. PLS. XXXVIII–XLI.—*West wall.*—There is a sketch of this wall by Bourgoin in PERR. and CHIP., *Histoire de l'Art: Égypte*, Fig. 115, which is useful as showing the general disposition. The scene of the table of offerings (on PL. XXXVIII, the top part on PL. XLI) is between two false doors, the one on the left being that represented on PL. XXXIX, and the one on the right being given on PL. XL. The left-hand door is inscribed, and also shows Ptah-hetep entering, walking out, being carried out, and sitting out of doors. At first sight this suggests that the door represents

[illegible] (There is shown on a very small scale in the [illegible] of the door [illegible] and more fully in the scene between the two doors (Pls. XXXVIII, XLI). The door on the right is not inscribed, but as the [illegible] towards Ptah-hetep from this direction it may be this door is intended for those leading into the court from the house itself, or else for one which leads into the kitchens, store-houses, etc. The study of the inscription on the left-hand door is to a great extent confirmatory of this view.

Left-hand door (Pl. XXXIX). (Düm., *Res.* I, pl. xiii).—This is sculptured in relief: at the top is the "cavetto" cornice (Perrot, *Dec. Art*, pp. 98–100), and below this is a narrow moulding which is carried also down the sides. Within the moulding are seen as it were two doorways, an outer and an inner, the jambs and architrave being in each case fully inscribed and sculptured. Between the two architraves is a broad space nearly filled with the scene of the table of offerings (as a "sign" or label indicating what goes on within), and below the lower architrave is seen the true lintel of rounded section. The double doorway is usual in such representations, and is evidently only an architectural development of a single doorway. In the earliest examples a single doorway is surmounted by the scene of the table of offerings, and the whole is surrounded by scenes. The "outer doorway" of the later instances may be interpreted therefore merely as a compact framing of the real doorway and the scene above. The whole stela or doorway is in the form of the "Divine Portal" of the inscription, which was presided over by Anubis (see first line of inscription on upper architrave and left jamb of inner doorway).

Inner doorway.—On the true lintel is written simply the name of Ptah-hetep. Directly above it his name is inscribed on the architrave, in the middle of the second of two lines of titles, etc., of which the signs face in opposite directions, outwards from the middle. On the right of his name Ptah-hetep is described as "deserving before the Great God," perhaps meaning Ra, and on the left as "deserving before Osiris." Both jambs are inscribed with prayers for Ptah-hetep, and the order in which these prayers are repeated on the architrave of the outer doorway shows that the prayer to Anubis on the left jamb is to be read first, followed by that to Osiris. *Left jamb.*—"May the King give an offering (or, grant grace), and may Anubis give an offering (or grant grace), who is chief of the Divine Portal, who is upon his hill, namely the (Ptah-hetep's) (?) burial [illegible] in *Kher-neter*, and [illegible] good old age, for (titles), the deserving before the Great God, Ptah-hetep." *Right jamb.*—"May the King give an offering and may Osiris give an offering, who is lord of Busiris chief of the western folk (the dead); that he may have funerary meals every day, for (titles), who loves Maat and is deserving before him, (titles), Ptah-hetep." At the end of each of these inscriptions is a figure of Ptah-hetep represented as though walking in or out through the doorway.

55. *Outer doorway.*—The horizontal inscription is closely similar to the inscriptions just translated, and is terminated by the same figure. 40

Right jamb.—In the order of events this inscription would seem to precede that on the left. "Crossing the water (or firmament?) in most excellent peace, coming out to the top of the noble of *Kher-neter*, the taking of his hand by his fathers and by his *ka*, each individual being worthy, a funerary offering being made to him at the top of the pit in his house of eternity, behold! that is an exceeding good old age before Osiris." At the end of this inscription we have Ptah-hetep seated in state under a light wooden canopy. Above and in front of him is a small figure of a priest holding a roll, and facing an inscription: "Is performed for him the tour; he is made *akh* by the lector in performing the ritual." The "tour" (*nemt*) apparently consists in his walking or being carried on his round of daily inspection. *Akh* denotes the qualities and powers proper to disembodied spirits, ghosts and genii. Almost the same inscription is over the table of offerings in the space between the two architraves.

Left jamb.—"Entering his house of eternity in most excellent peace, he being in a state of worthiness before Anubis, at the head of *Kher-neter*, after he has received funerary offerings at the top of the pit, after the tour, after the service of making him *akh* by the lectors, by reason of his exceeding great favour before the king and Osiris." At the foot of this inscription we have Ptah-hetep carried, seated on a throne under a light wooden canopy which is conveyed on the shoulders of four men. These canopies show that the scenes are supposed to take place in the open, where shelter is required from the sun.

It seems then that the whole door represents the "Divine Portal," over which Anubis presides, and which is the entrance to the realm of the dead and of the gods. Its inscriptions show that of Anubis were demanded burial and a "good old age," and the latter term is explained as connoting practically facilities for movement to different places of advantage in the blessed land, and the help of such ministrations as were to enable the deceased to enjoy the luxuries and necessities of earthly life in the world beyond the grave. For the actual provisions, however, which are to keep him from suffering hunger there, he appeals to Osiris, the ruler of the land and chief of the Western Dead. It is remarkable that an appeal to the king almost invariably precedes that to any gods. The king in question is doubtless always the Pharaoh who happens to be reigning at any time when the prayer is repeated; probably his sanction and assistance were in theory required towards every benefit desired by any of his subjects, whether dead or alive, on earth, or in the under world, or even in heaven.

The scene of the table of offerings is given in epitome on the tablet over the inner doorway, but we have a much fuller version of it on the same wall (PLS. XXXVIII, XLI, DÜM., *Res.* I, xii–xiii). In the pyramids of Unas and Pepy II, there is given the full ritual of this great funerary scene: this M. Maspero has lately expounded on various occasions; he has also just issued a full explanation of it in the *Revue de l'Histoire des Religions*, vols. xxxv–vi. In the present instance we shall simply describe the scene as here represented.

Ptah-hetep is seated before a table of offerings: he wears a wig and false beard, and is clothed with a panther's skin—the claws and tail of which are visible—fastened with an elegant tie over the left shoulder. He is raising a jar of unguent to his face. Under his throne-chair kneels or squats a small figure unfinished. Above him is an inscription giving his titles as priest of the pyramids of Assa, of Ne-User-Ra and of Men-kau-her. Before him is a table of offerings to which servants are still bringing additions, and above it and them is a detailed list of offerings and ceremonies connected with it (PL. XLI); the purification of the table, the incense, unguents, foods, etc. (See Maspero's articles.)

On PL. XXXVIII there are four rows of officiating persons. In the upper row are the priests, washing the slab of purification, burning incense and reciting services. The three rows below represent persons of somewhat high standing, bringing offerings.

56. The second false door (roughly sketched on PL. XL) is unusual. Certain coloured sketches of details made by Miss Pirie show that the elaborately coloured plates in PERROT and CHIPIEZ (*L'Égypte*, pls. xiii, xiv and p. 792) are in the main correct, although by no means absolutely so. In the French work the door itself is represented as made of wooden panels, and around the door the broader vertical spaces are filled with patterns imitating that work in checkers and chevrons of colour. These mats are held down at the base by cords passed through loops. The narrower spaces are filled with patterns having the appearance of chains, which the French writers believe to represent actual chains used for pulling up the mats or curtains. They seem, however, rather to represent loops at the sides of the mats for holding them in place by means of rods or cords passed through the loops, which would also perhaps serve for raising or lowering the matwork. At the bottom these loops fall together in a heap, while above they are stretched fully apart.

PTAH-HETEP.

57. Since Ptah-hetep was priest at the pyramids of Ne-user-Ra, Men-kau-her, and Assa,—three successive kings towards the end of the Vth dynasty—, we may consider him as belonging to the reign of King Assa. From his tomb we learn that his two "elder sons" were named Akhet-hetep and Ptah-hetep. There are many Ptah-heteps of this time, the most celebrated being the composer of the Proverbs, who is said to have been the eldest son of a king, and grand *waztr*. It is a curious fact that in MAR., *Mast.* pp 350 *et seqq.*, there is described the tomb of a Ptah-hetep of about the same period, likewise having an elder son "named Akhet-hetep; probably this Ptah-hetep was the "elder son" of our Ptah-hetep. He was "chief architect of the king," *i.e.* presumably of Unas, and the sculpture of his tomb is highly praised by Mariette. Akhet-hetep, the other "elder son" of our Ptah-hetep, is probably to be recognised in the owner of the tomb described by MAR., *Mast.* p. 421, and who was priest of the pyramid of Unas, the successor of Assa.

Ptah-hetep's titles and epithets are as follows. He was (PLS. XXXI, XXXIII, XXXV, XLI) "governor of the pyramid city," "enlightener of the priests of the pyramid 'Nefer' of Assa, of the *uab* priests of the pyramid 'Men-sut,' of Ne-user-Ra, and of the priests of the pyramid 'Neter-sut' of Men-kau-her." It will be observed that Assa, [illegible] successfully [illegible] in the [illegible] (Pls. XXXII [illegible] and XXXIII) "[illegible] after the king," "[illegible] of the enlightened people (?)," "filling of the mother's [illegible]," "[illegible] Archer of Hekt" (the frog goddess), "traverser of the deserts (?)," "captain of the (royal?) [illegible]," "inspector of canals of the southern [illegible] (?)," "priest of Maat, giver of commands to the land-holders (?), governor of the Great House, director of the great court (cf. Pl. XXXIX), director of [illegible], charged with the hearing of petitions (?), chief of the secrets of all commands of the king, worthy before the great god, Osiris, and Anubis, chief of the Western Dead." In the large inscription of Pls. XLI, XXXVIII, he is also "worthy before the king" and "Captain of [illegible] of the Southern Tens." In another place (Pl. XXXIX) he is "priest of Maat, whom the king loves," and "one who loves Maat, and deserving before her"—Maat being, of course, the goddess of Truth and Justice. It is very tempting to see in this exalted and high-minded official the composer of the *Proverbs* of Ptah-hetep, which he spake before the king Assa.

The titles of other officials which appear in this tomb are mostly obscure, and perhaps not much that is profitable could at present be learned from them. Time and space are at any rate both lacking to consider them here.

Mariette in his *Mastabas*, p. 359, gives the plan of a tomb entitled "D. 64, Ptah-hotep II," without further information. Professor Petrie points out that the measurement and direction of the final chamber agree tolerably well with those of our tomb, and that "D. 64" may therefore be identical with this. He also suggests that the reason Mariette treated this fine tomb with such marked brevity in his notes was that he intended to have a full copy and description prepared later. Professor Petrie is undoubtedly right in the identification. Bourgoin's copy of the W. wall gives 5·2 m. for the length of the chamber; this is within 6 in. of the 5·34 m. of "D. 64." Our Pls. XXXI, XXXII give for the E. wall 203 in., *i.e.* only two inches less than Bourgoin's measurement of the opposite wall. The latter is more difficult to measure on our plates. The breadth of the chamber in "D. 64" is 2·18 m. (= 86 in.), as against about 80–84 in. in our plates, where the deficit can of course be explained by the probability that the edges are for a short distance blank.

The identification is also confirmed by the valuable *Carte de la nécropole memphite*, newly published by M. de Morgan, pl. x. of which shows, lying west of the Step Pyramid at Saqqareh, tombs in the following order: *Ra-duа-n* (evidently D. 61 of *Mast.*); *Ptah-hotep* (D. 62), probably of a son of our Ptahhotep, see above p. 33; *Atta* (D. 63); then another *Ptah-hotep*, agreeing with our tomb as marked in Baedeker's map, and evidently "D. 64." D. 61–64 are stated to be in the *Zone de l'Ouest*; see *Mast.*, p. 65. We may here note that E. 17 (*l.c.* p. 421), the tomb of that Akhethotep whom we take to be the elder son of our Ptahhotep, is apparently the *Khuthotep* of de Morgan's map, lying apart, south-east of the Step Pyramid (*cf. Mast.*, p. 67).

According to Mariette the axis of "D. 64" is 15° east of the magnetic North. The mastaba measures 80½ × 63 ft. It contains four chambers, of which the one here published is the innermost, and was reached through a long entrance passage and two chambers; one of these was 20 feet square and had a roof supported by two pillars. It is further stated (p. 359) that "D. 65," the tomb of the princess Ra-hent, is built against the east wall of "D. 64."

ERRATA TO PLATES.

Dümichen's copy occasionally supplies a few signs and details that have been destroyed, and are therefore not to be found in the present work.

Pl. XXXII.—According to the photograph in Mar., *Voyage* the ground line in the 3rd row should be continued to the end.

Pl. XXXIII.—Top row. The second arm of the captive, and the cord above the elbow, should be inserted, as in the hieroglyph of the captive; an arm of one of the soldiers in the same scene is also missing (see the description).

INDEX.

PAGE

Aahmes 16
Addax antelope 30
Akh 32
Akhom, hawk 9, 15
Alabaster, tub of 11
Altar 8
Amenhotep II 5, 15
„ III 5
„ IV 15
Anna 5
Aputh 21
Arches 7
Artist's signature 29
Aupuat 21

Balanites 3
Beads 12
Beba 5, 15
Bek oil 16
Bird-catching 29
Bitumen 10
Boat-building 29
Book of Dead 11
Bourgoin 31
Boy in ivory 3
Brick stamps 15
Bubale 28
Buffoons 15
Butchers 31

Cages 29
Cambridge 10
Canopic vases 11, 17
Cartonnage 10, 18
Castanets 3
Cement 10
Chambers of brick 2
Chapels, XXIInd dynasty . 8
Cheta 13
Christie, Mr. 2

PAGE

Clap-nets 28
Coins, Ptolemaic 13
Counters of gifts 18

Dama, antelope 30
Dancer in wood 3
Decoys in hunting 28
Deir-el-bahri 4, 5
Dolls 3
Dôm palm 3
Doorway in tomb 32
Dümichen 26
Dwarfs 27

Erman, Professor 29
Estate names 30, 31
Examining meat 31

False doors 17, 32
„ „ double 26
Foundation deposits . . . 5, 6
Funerary chapels 11

Games 27
Gazelle 28
Geese, three kinds 30
Girgis 1
Glazing, method of . . . 3
Goose and ibis 18
Griffith, Miss 2

Hares 29
Hartmann 26
Haworth, J., Mr. 2
Hawk, wooden 9
Heart scarabs 12
Hedgehog 28
Henu bark 16
Hoopoe 27
Horakhti 11, 17

PAGE

Hor of Edfu 16
Hor-se-ast 8, 18
House 1
Hyaena 29

Ibex 28
Ichneumon 28
Incense 16
Iron 4
„ axe 13
„ date of 13
Ivory boy 3

Jerboa 28

Kadesh 5
Karama 17
Kennard, M., Mr. 2

Lapis lazuli 12
Leather braces 3
Leopard skin 5
Library Ramesseum . . . 2

Mariette 26
Maspéro, G., Professor . . 33
Mat door 33
Mehenk 28
Menat 10
Method of work 2
Milne, J. G., Mr. . . . 2, 13
Mimusops 10
Min 16
Mohassib, M. 1
Mortars 8
Murray, Miss 2, 31
Mutardas 18

Nails, wooden 10
Neferhetep 8, 15

	PAGE
Nekht-ef-Mut	10, 16, 18
Nekht-min	8
Nemauroth	12
Nitre	4
Nomes in O. K.	30
Nut	17
Oil jars	15
Oryx	28, 30
Osorkon I	10, 16
Ostraca	15
Papyrus XIIth dynasty	3
„ gathering	27
Paget, Miss	25
Panther's skin	33
Pens of reed	3
Perrot and Chipiez	26
Pilgrim bottle	13
Pillars, low level	5
Pirie, Miss	2, 4, 8, 25
Plaster	7
Prayer to King	33
Ptah-hetep, life	33
Quails	30
Quftis	1
Rames	8
Rameses II at Deir-el-bahri	5
„ Foundation deposits	6
Rameses III	9
Resin	10
Re-use of tomb	3, 4
Rougé, de	25
Sacrifice, human	14
Salad-mixers	4
Scarabs, heart	12
„ lazuli	12
Seals	8
Sebek-hetep II	5
Sehetep-ab-ra	13
Sekhet	7
Set	15
Sethef	27
Sety I	9
„ II	9
Shep-en-sepdet	12
Sheshanq	12
Silver	11
Sipairi	5, 20
Slughi dogs	28, 29
Spears, bronze	8
Statues, pottery	5
„ mud	8
Stelae, wood	10, 11, 18
Stela unfinished	19
Swans	30
Table of offering	33
Teknu	14
Tep-res	14
Tharu	16
Thieving	1
Thompson, H., Mr.	2
Thoth, feast	30
Thothmes II	16
„ III	5
„ IV	5, 15
Toilet scene	27
Tomb wells	2
Tree goddess	8
Trial pieces	9
Tribute	29, 31
Trichonema	11
Tuy	9
Unet	19
Ushabtis	12
Vineyard scene	28
Wakf	30
Walker, Dr.	2
Whidborne, Miss	2
White ants	10
Wild cattle	28
„ dogs	28
Wine pressing	28
„ seals	16
Wrestling	29
Zed-mut-es-ankh	11

LONDON: PRINTED BY WILLIAM CLOWES AND SONS, LIMITED, STAMFORD STREET AND CHARING CROSS.

1:400 THEBES. PLAN OF RAMESSEUM. I.

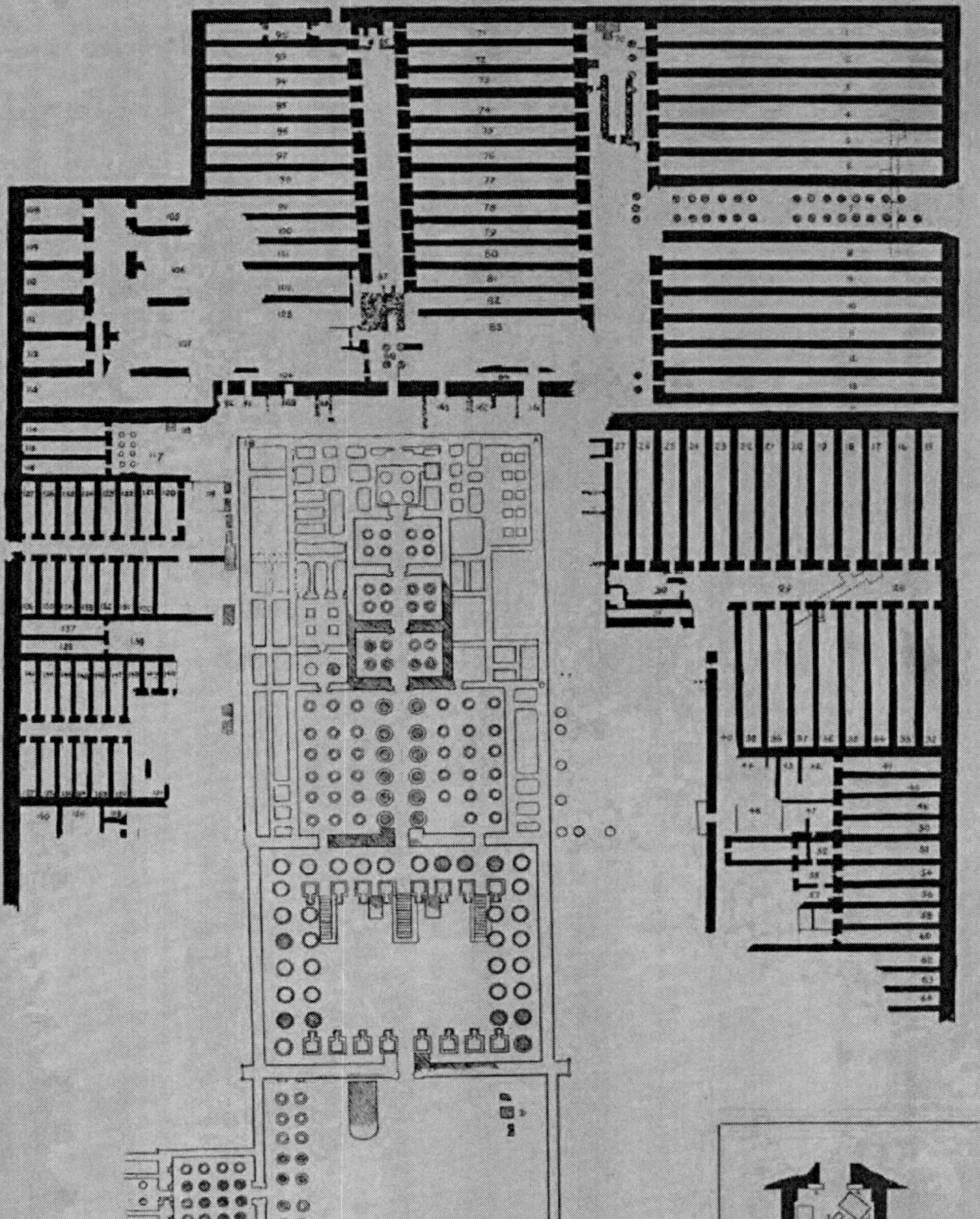

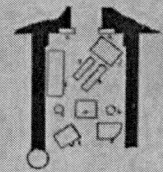

1 : 2

THEBES. XIITH DYNASTY TOMB. RAMESSEUM.

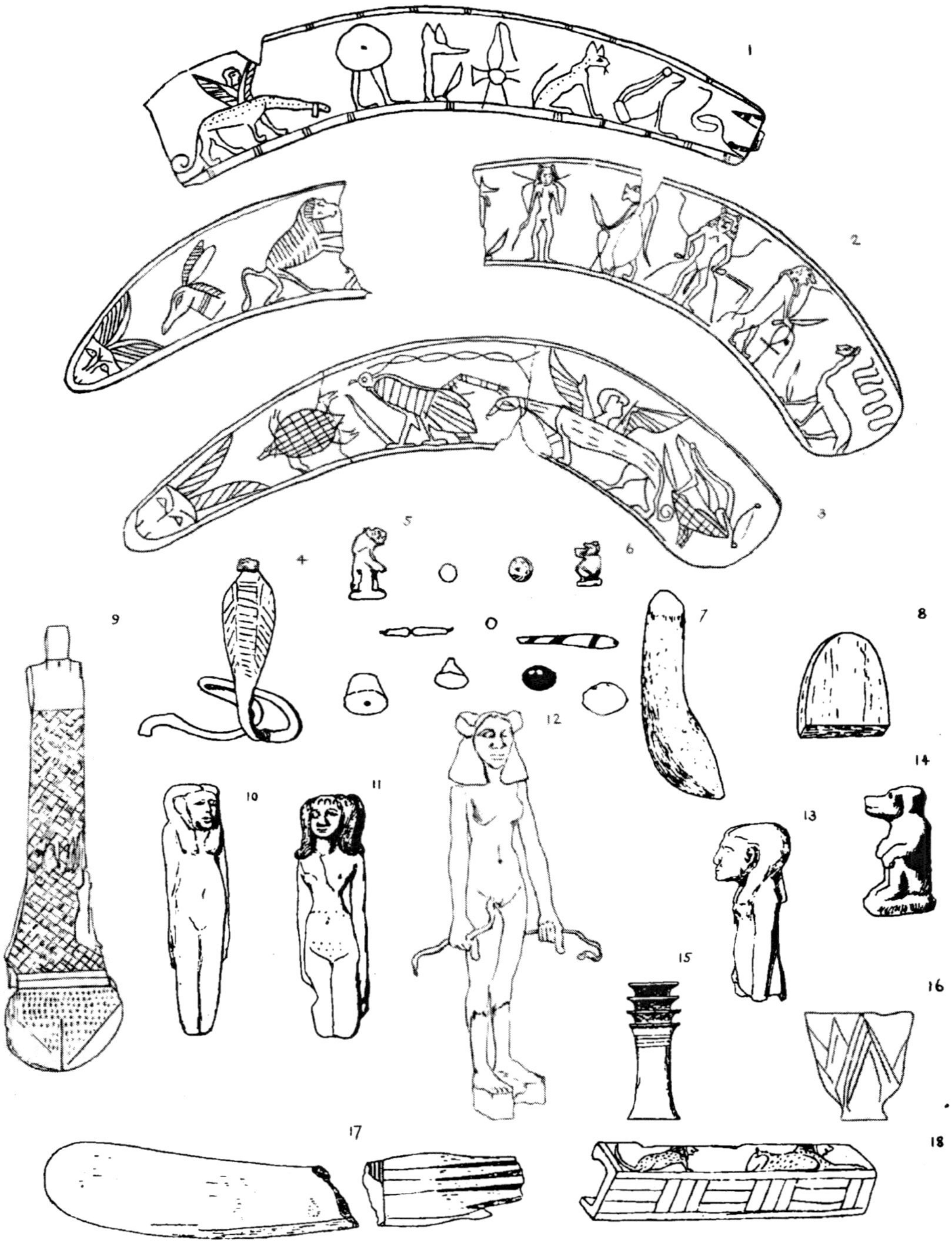

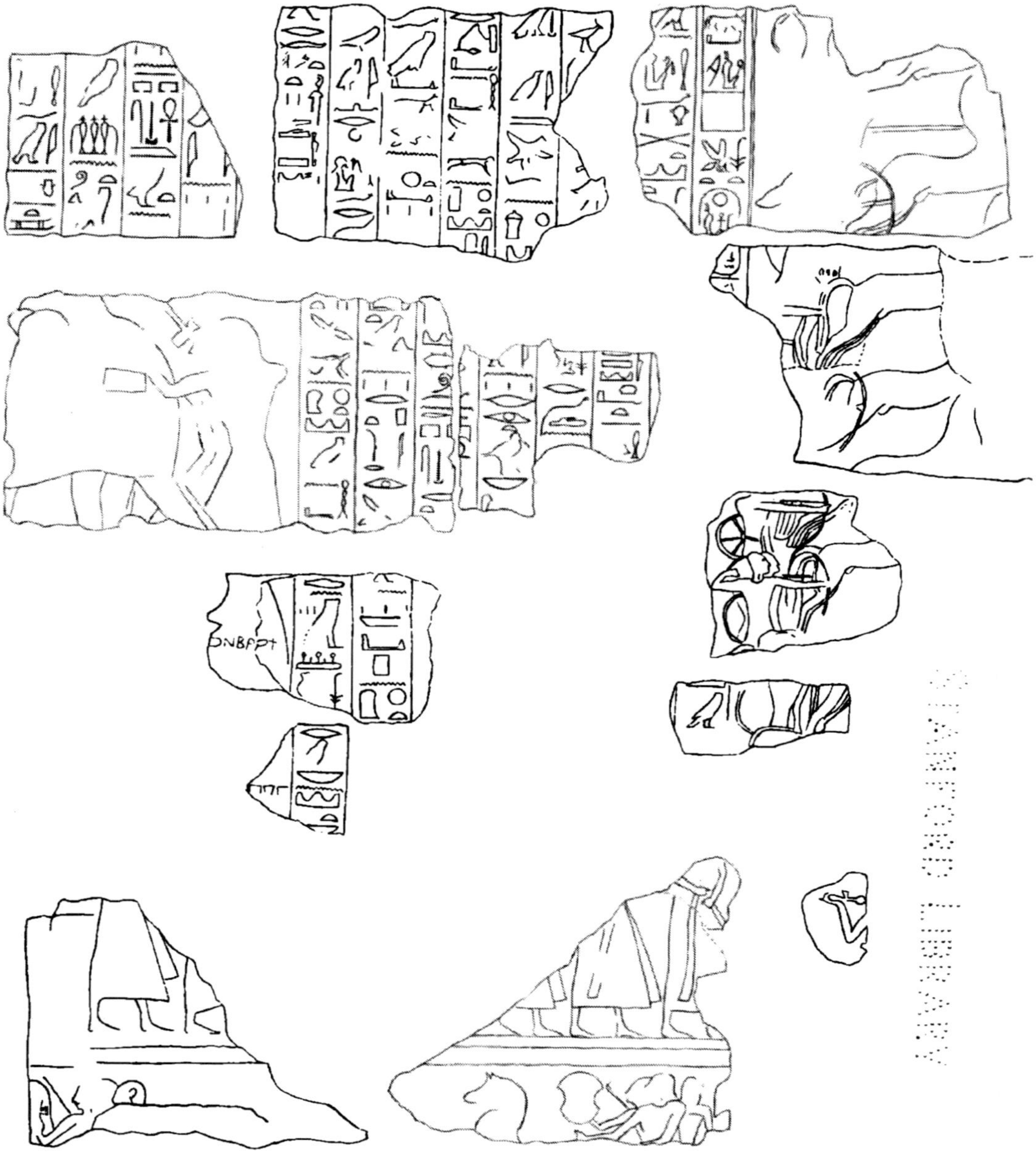

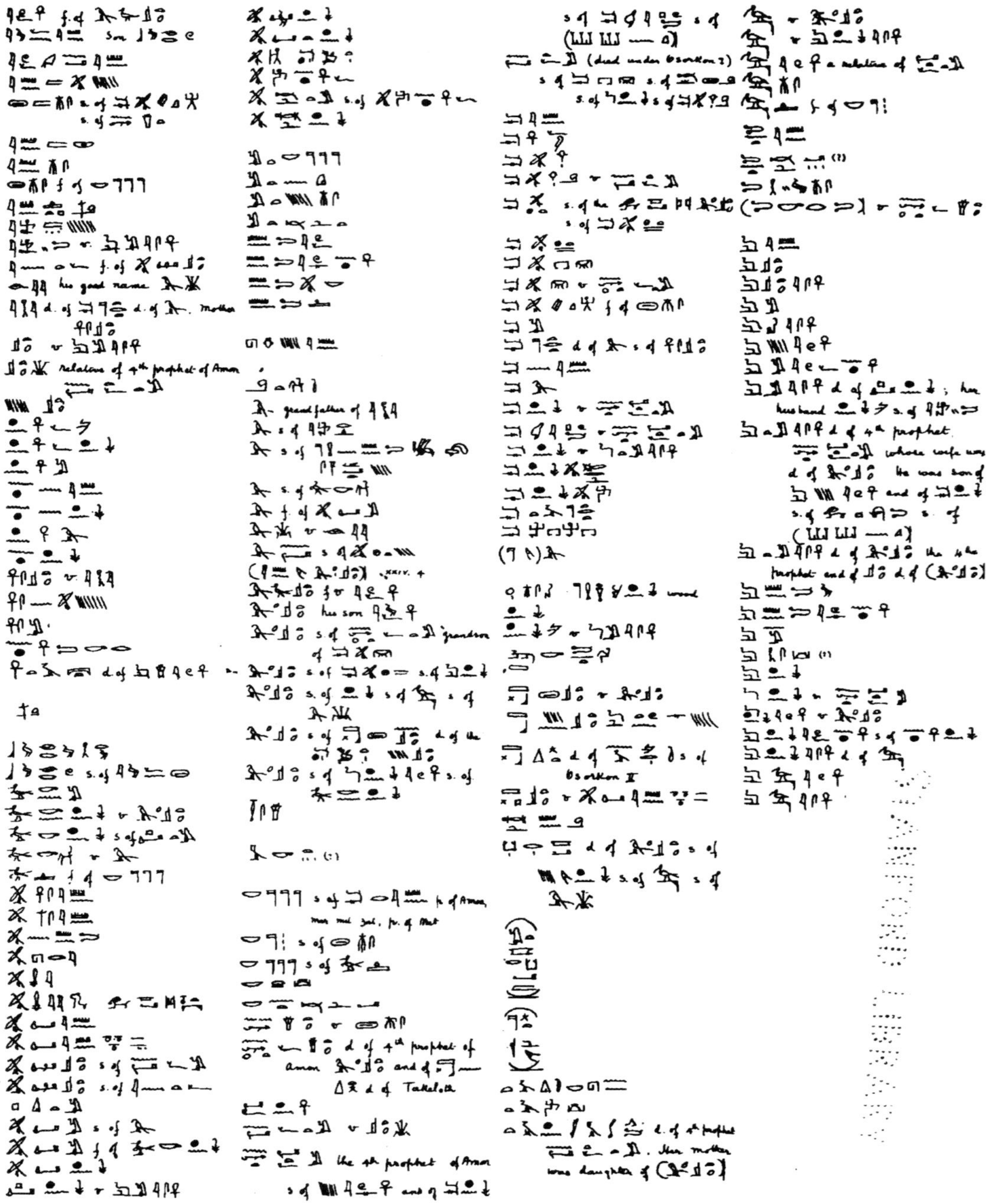
his good name
relative of 4th prophet of Amon
grandfather of
his son
grandson of
(dead under Osorkon 2)
Osorkon II
the 4th prophet of Amon
d. of 4th prophet of Amon
d. of Takeloth
Her mother was daughter of
d. of 4th prophet
whose wife was
He was son of
the 4th prophet

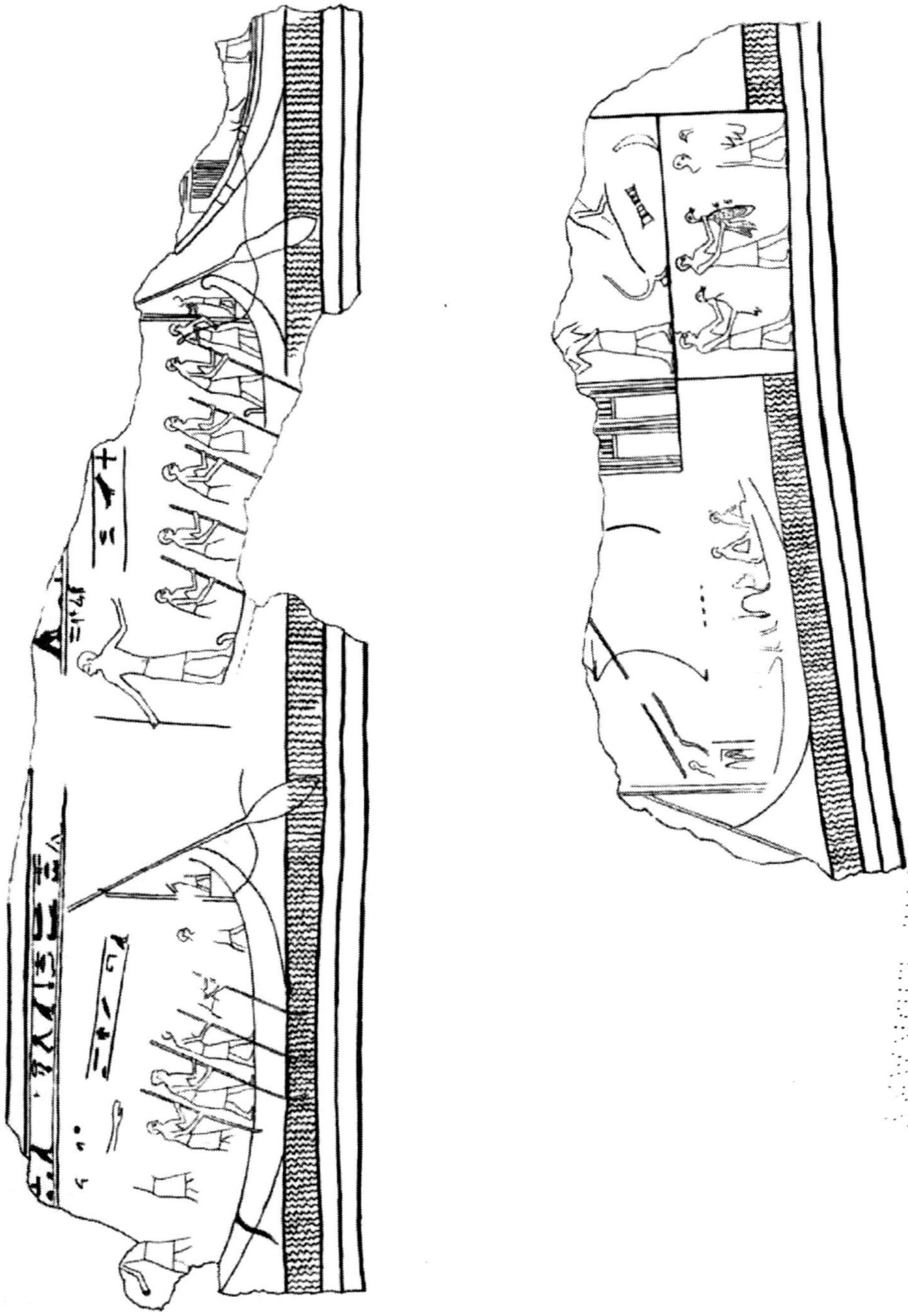

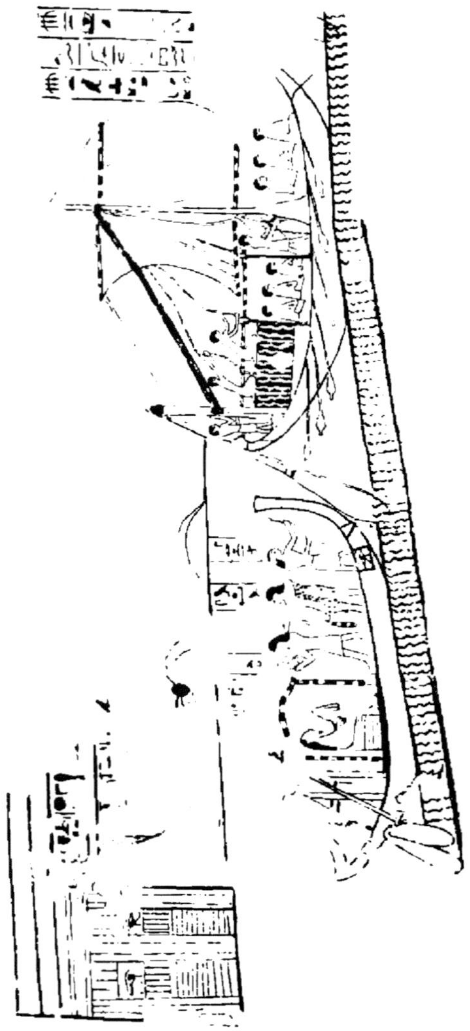

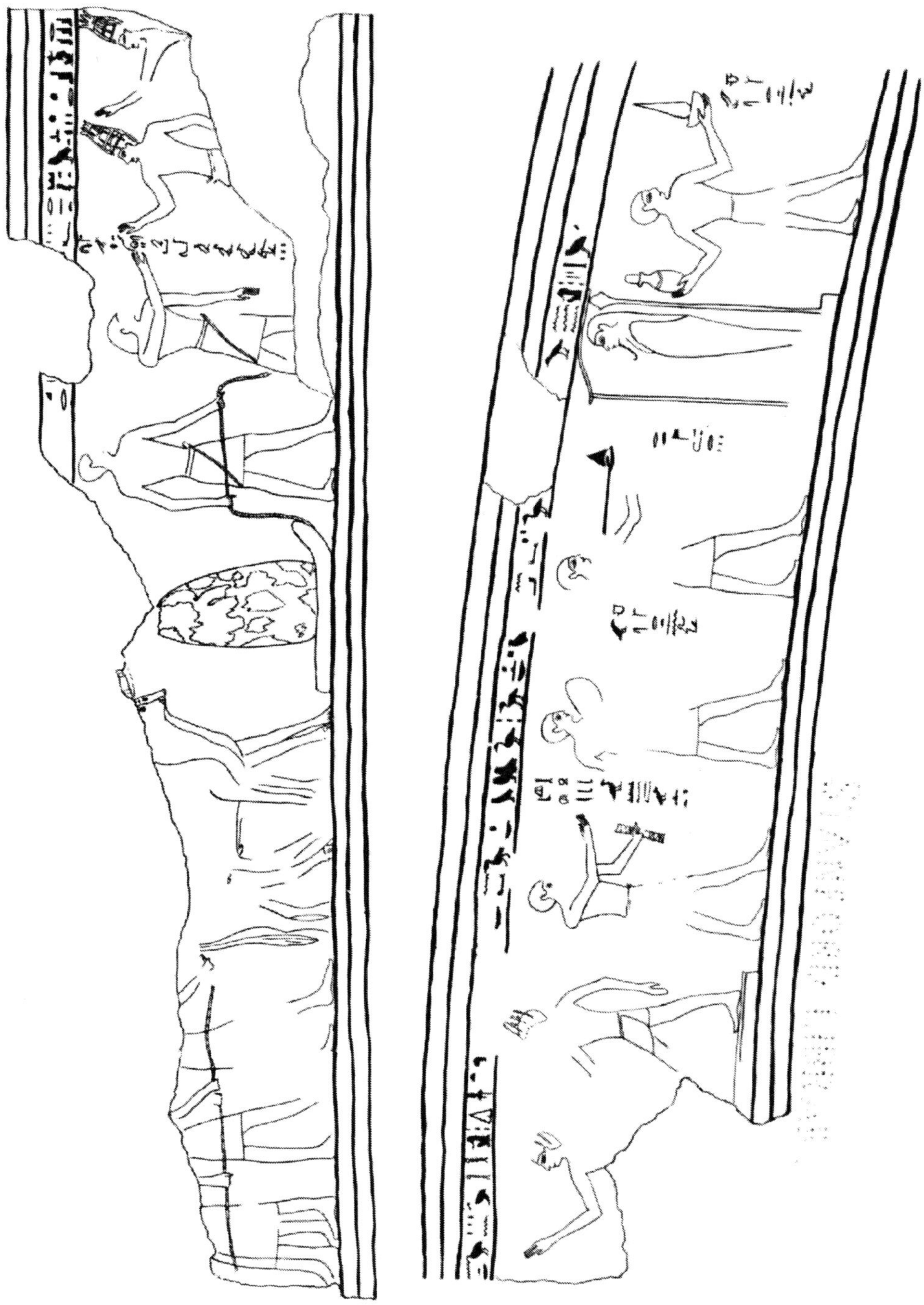

1 2 3 4 5 6 7 8
9 10 11 12 13 14 15 16 17 18
19 20 21 22 23 24 25 26 27 28
29 30 31 32 33 34 35 36 37
38 39 40 41 42 43 44 45 46 47 48 49

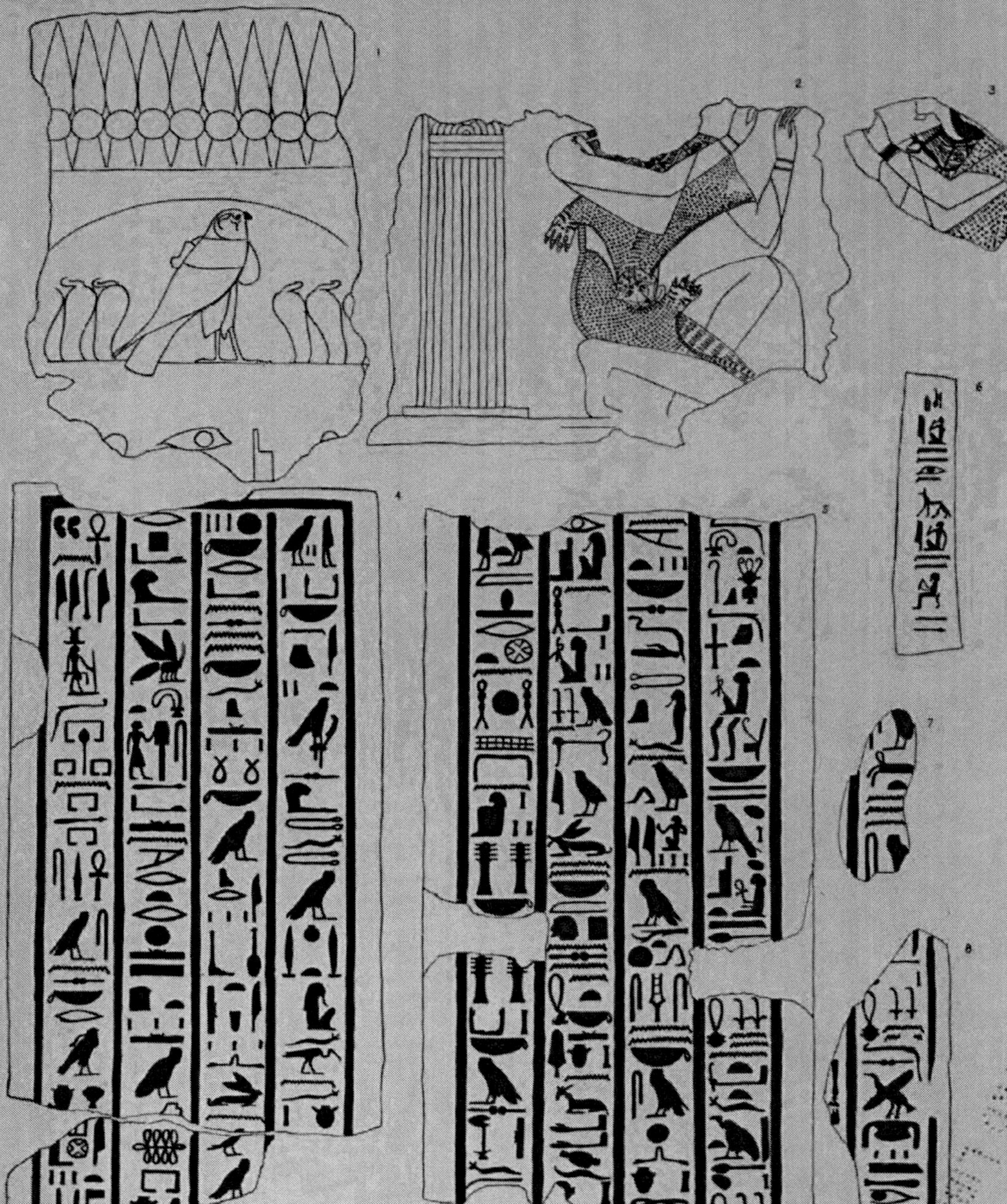

1
2
3
4
5
6

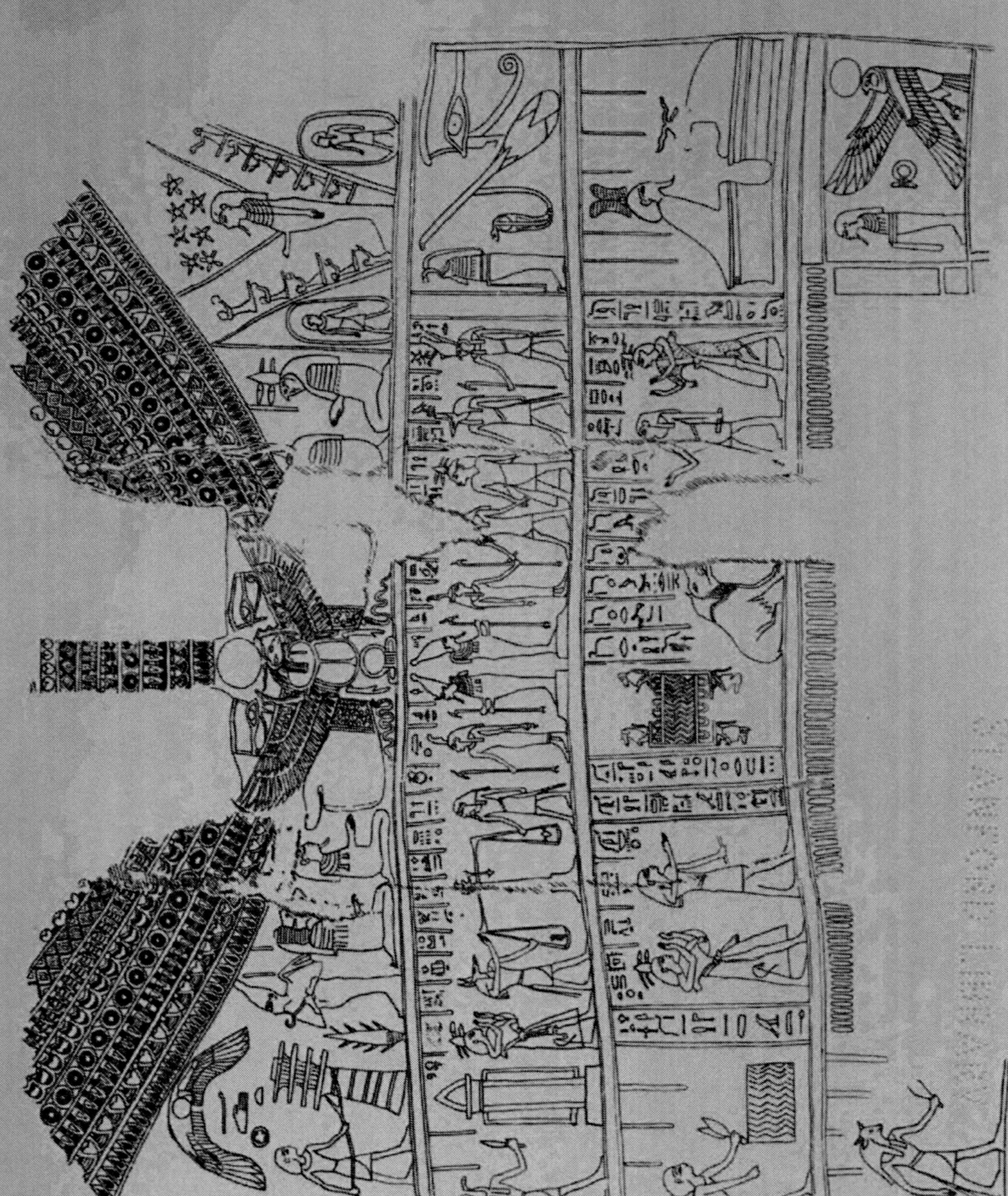

1

2

3

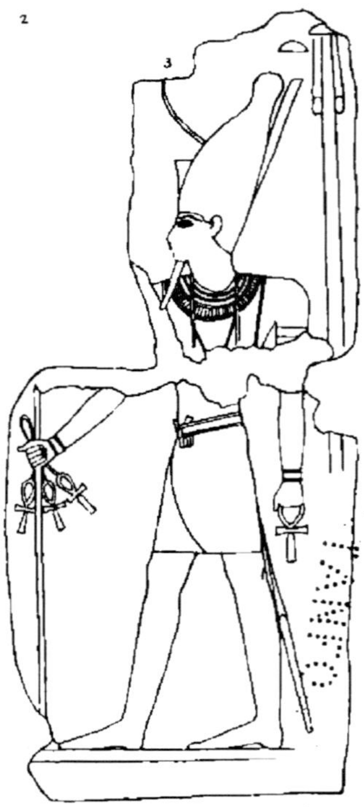

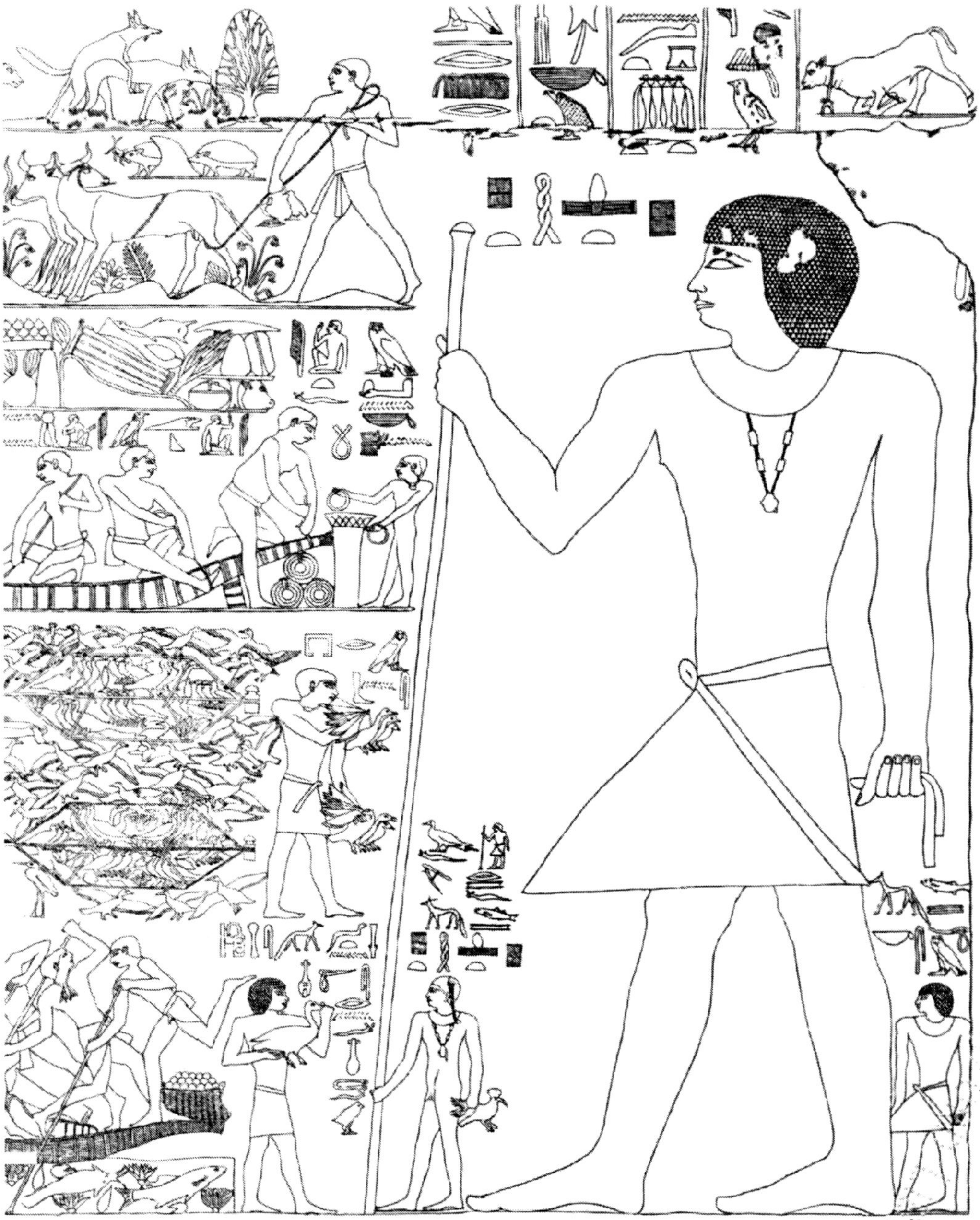

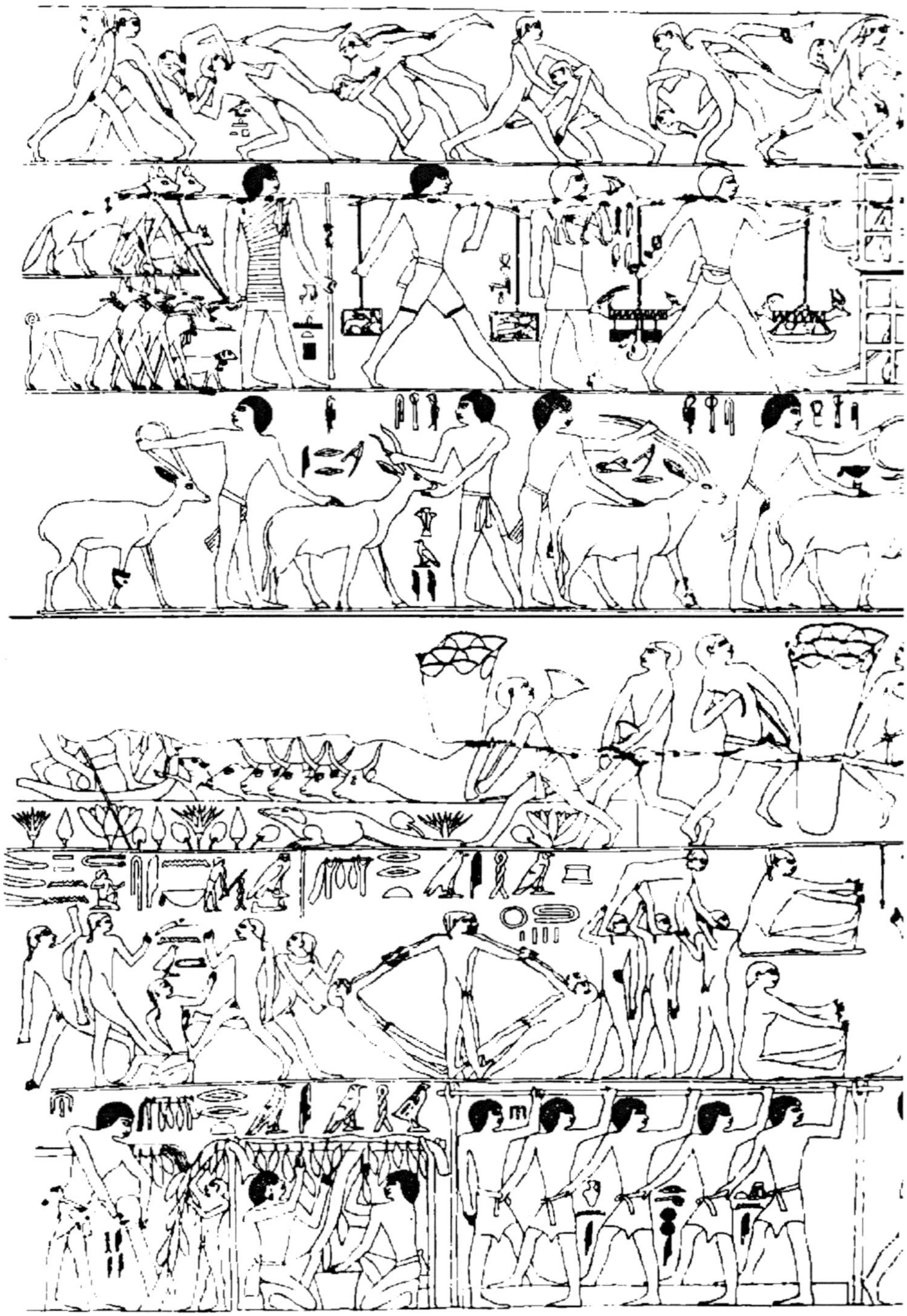

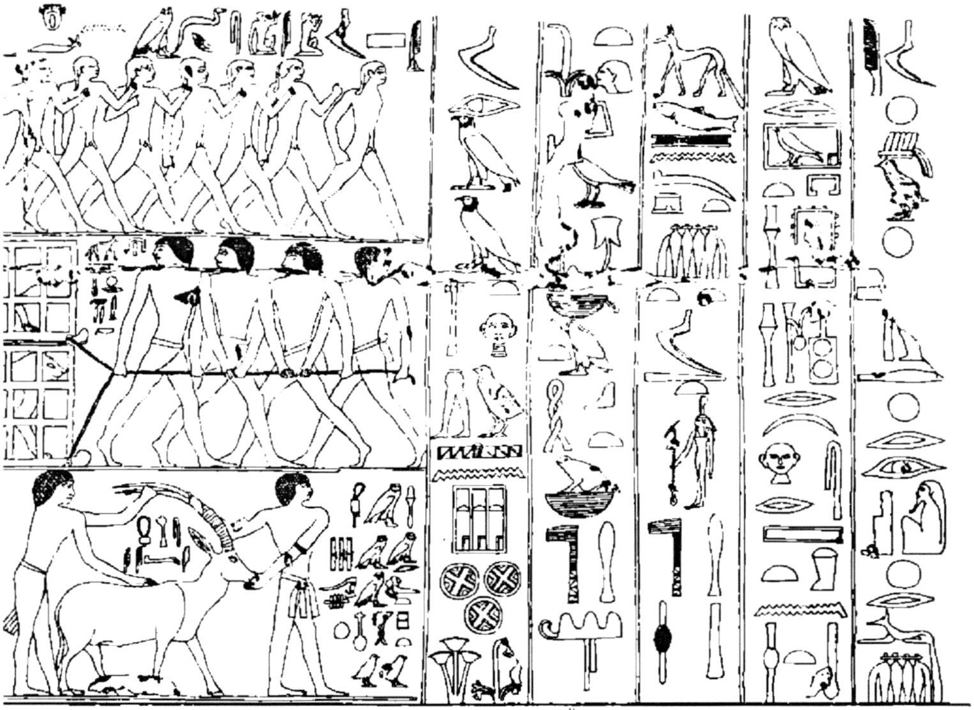

S. WALL. TOP. W. END. ABOVE PL. XXXI.

S. WALL. TOP, E. END. ABOVE PL. XXXII.

XXXV. top hal

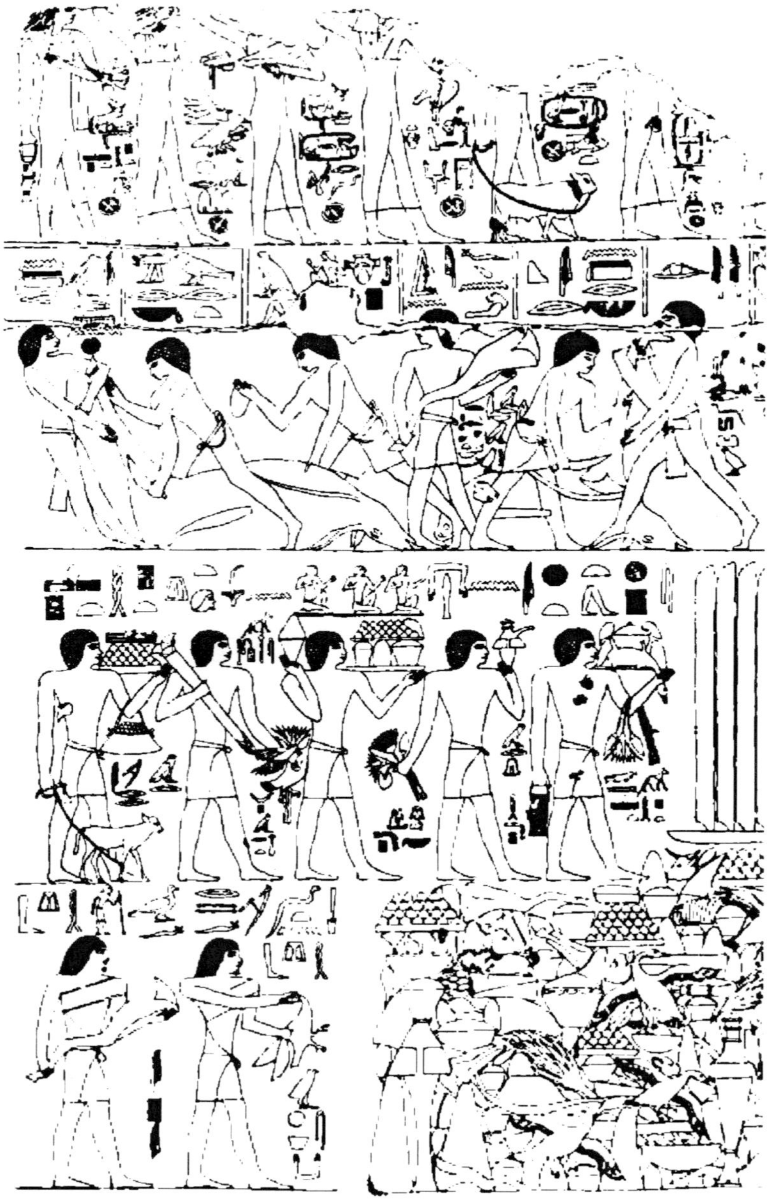

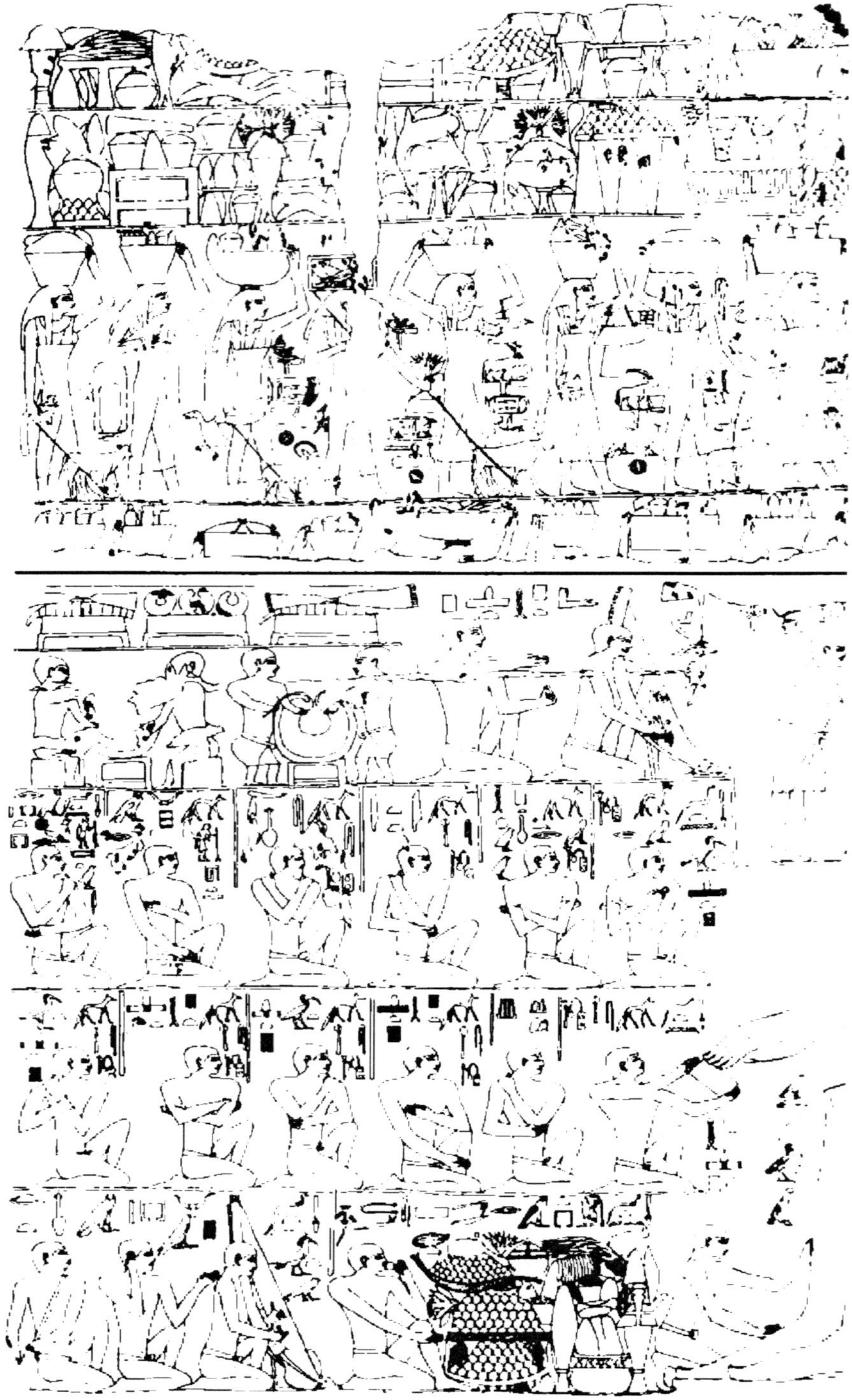

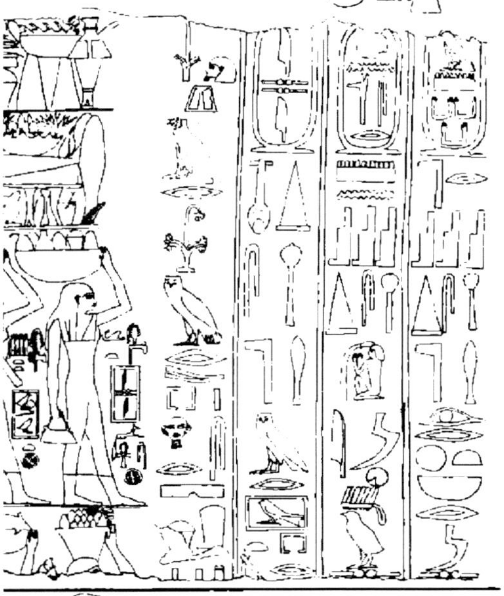

W. END.

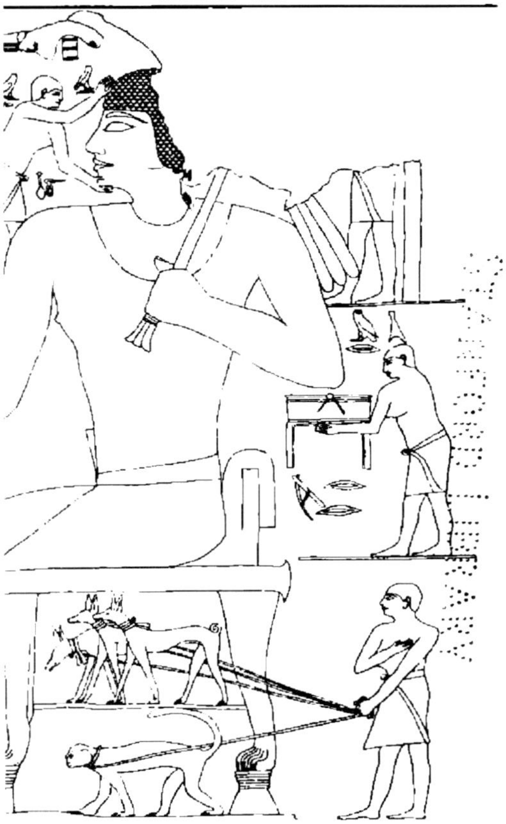

E. END. ABOVE THE DOOR.

Here Pl. XXXV

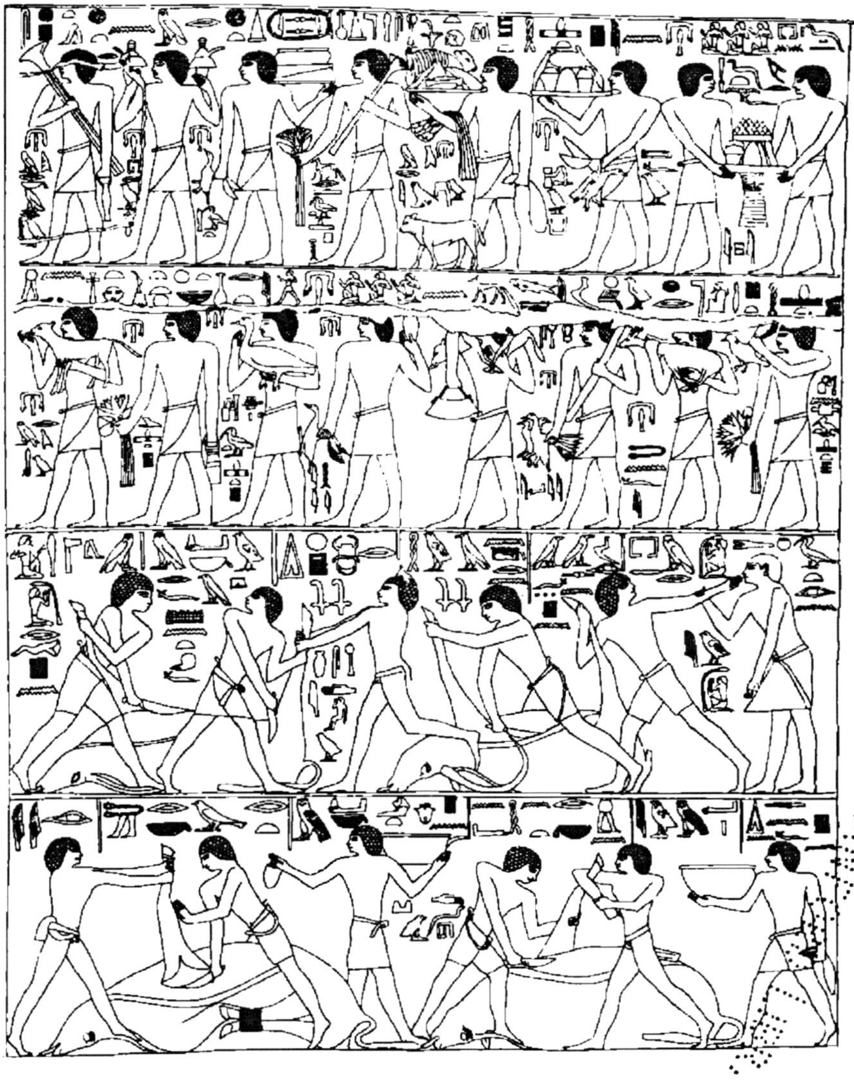

Plate XLI. above

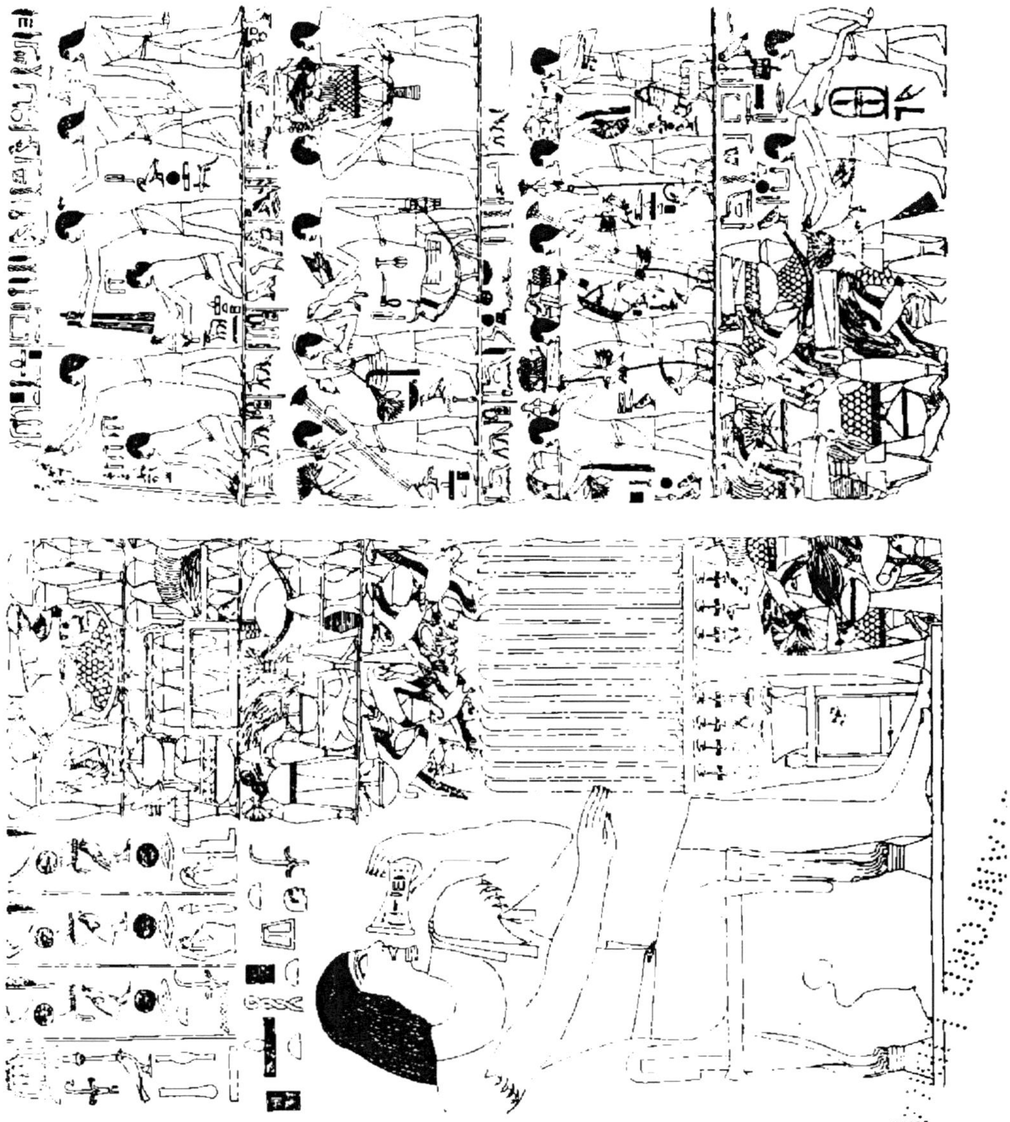

1:10 SAQQARA. TOMB OF PTAH-HOTEP, N. WALL, W. FALSE DOOR. XXXIX.

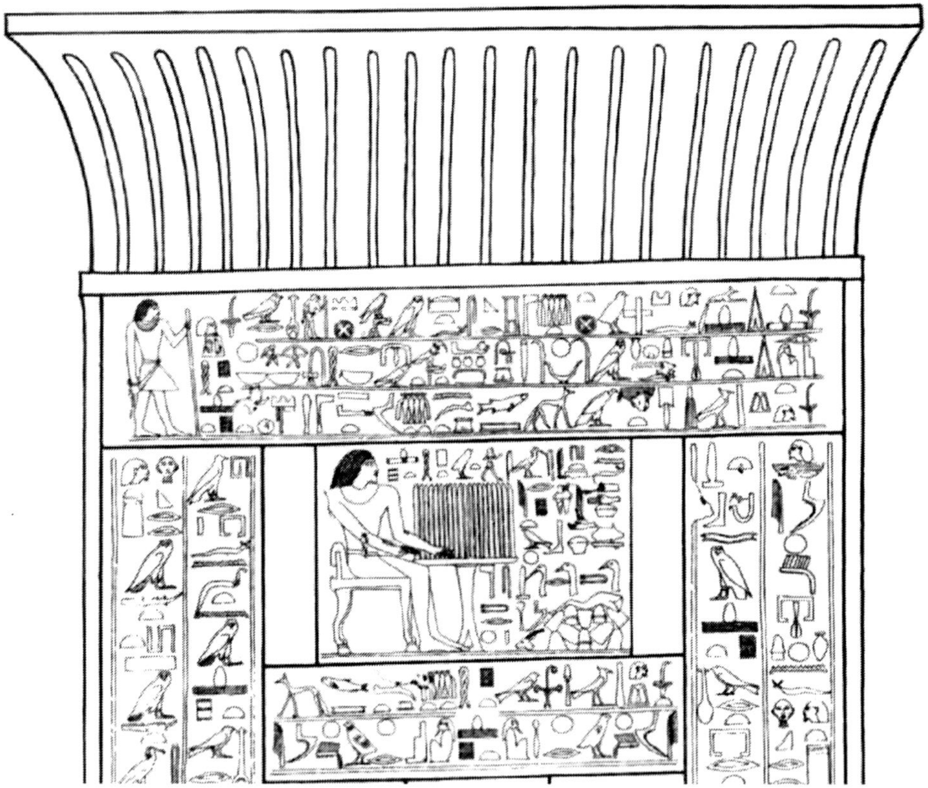

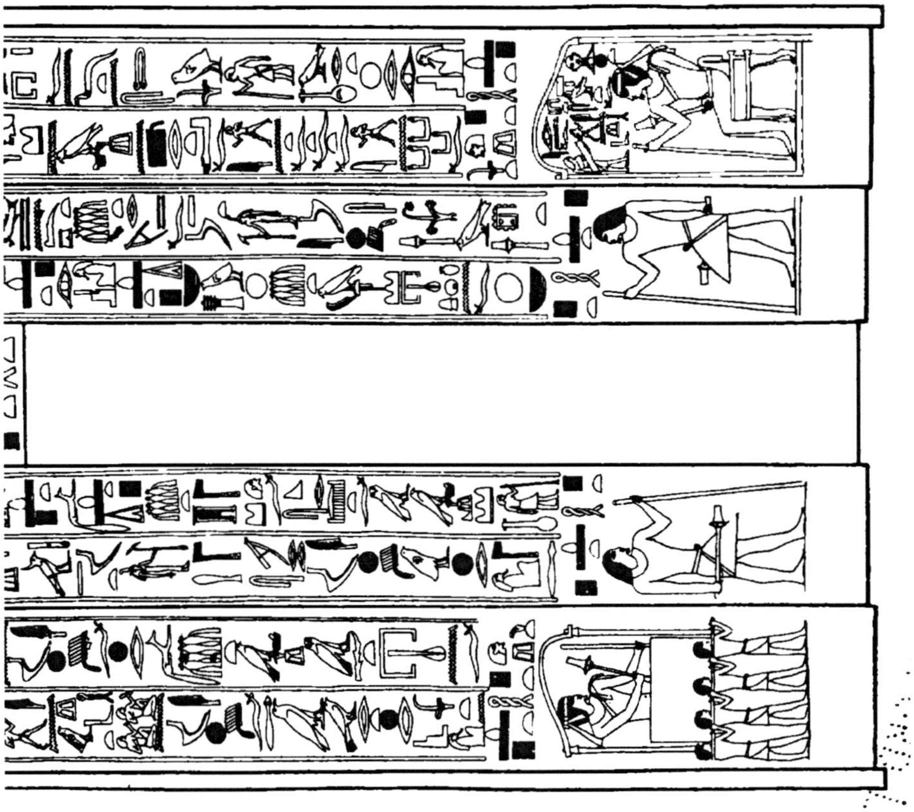

1:12 SAQQARA. TOMB OF PTAH-HOTEP, N. WALL, E. DOOR. XL.

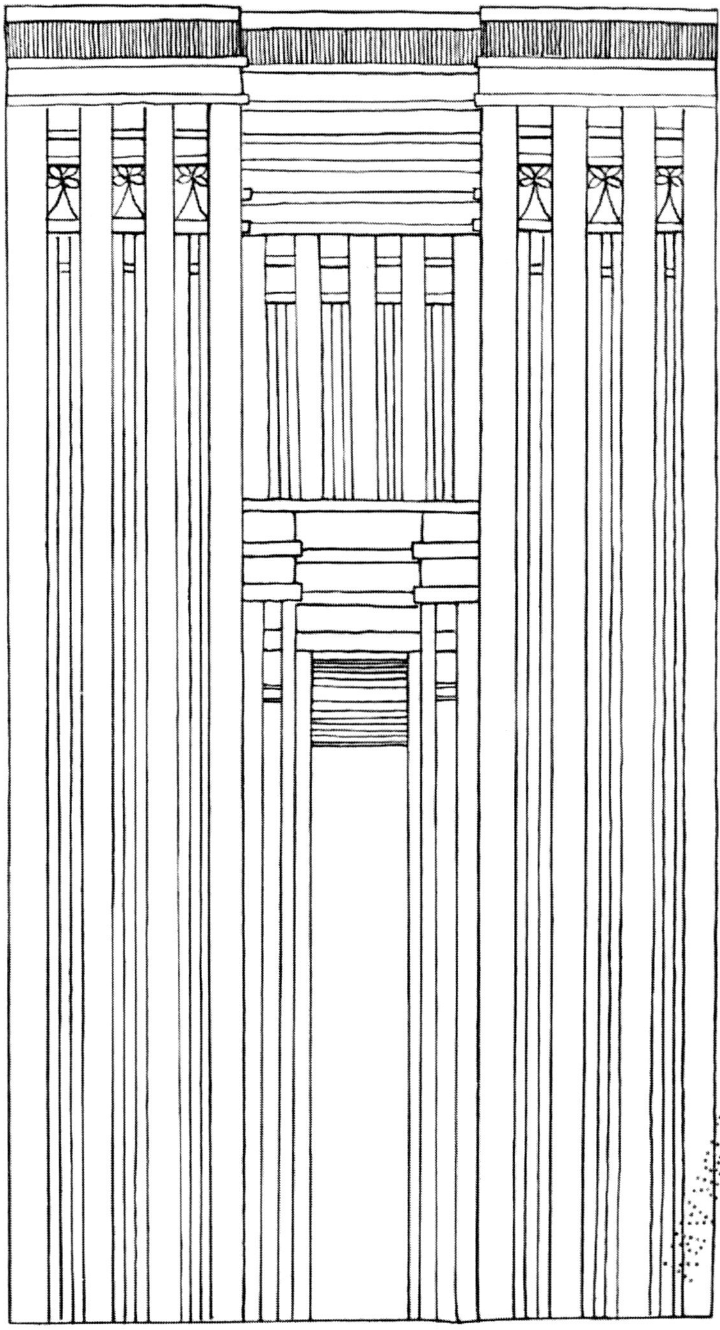

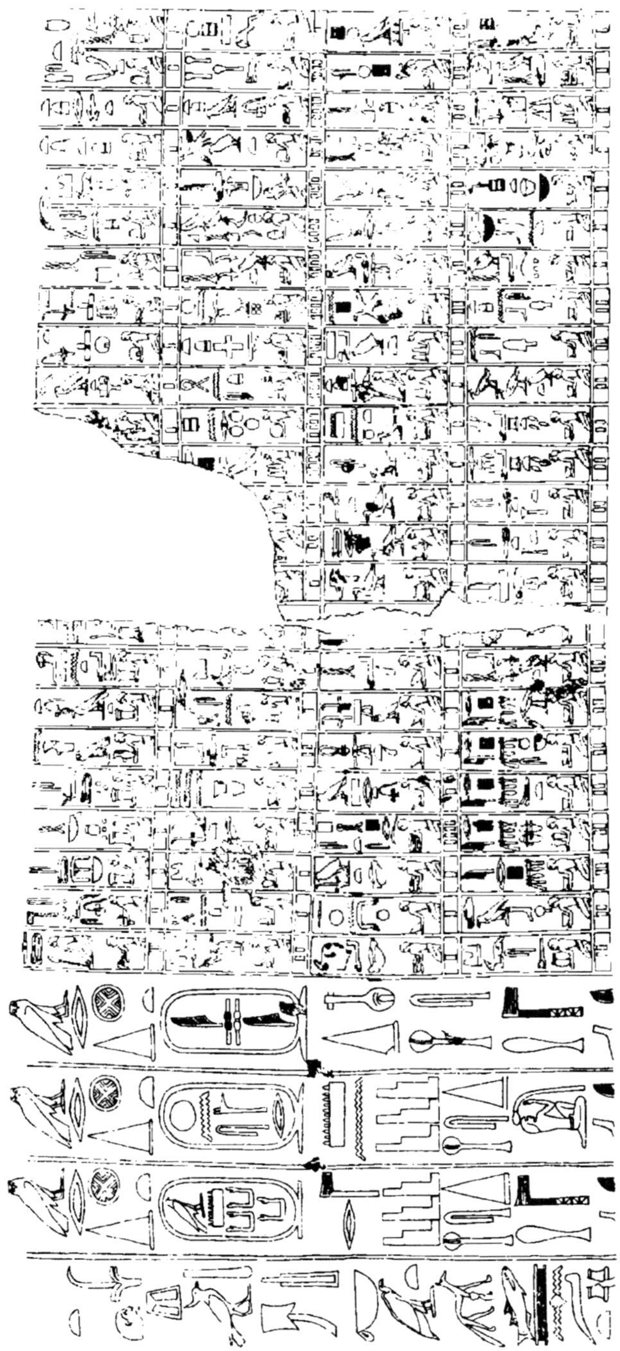

Plate XXXVIII. below

Lightning Source UK Ltd.
Milton Keynes UK
UKOW012312060712

195608UK00004B/38/P